DAZED AND CONFUSED

Inspired by
the screenplay by Richard Linklater

Compiled by Richard Linklater,
Denise Montgomery, and friends.

St. Martin's Griffin ≉ New York

Design by Erik Josowitz, Zero-G Design

Library of Congress Cataloging-in-Publication Data

Linklater, Richard
     Dazed and Confused / Richard Linklater
         p.   cm.
     ISBN 0-312-09466-3
     1. Dazed and confused (Motion picture) 2. United States--Popular culture.
     3. Motion pictures--Social aspects--United States.
     I. Title.
     PN1997.D343L56 1993
     791.43'72--dc20   93-868
                                      CIP

FIRST EDITION: SEPTEMBER 1993
10 9 8 7 6 5 4 3

ACKNOWLEDGMENTS

I would like to thank our intrepid editor at St. Martin's Press, Jim Fitzgerald, and our stalwart book agent, Stephen Pevner, both of whom valiantly supported the "book crew" as we relived our high school experiences throughout the production of this book. Special thanks to Nancy Cushing-Jones at M.C.A., Tricia Linklater, and Ron Marks for helping this process run smoothly. Thanks to the folks at Gramercy Pictures: Russell Schwarz, Claudia Gray, Steve Flynn and Allison Allen for their belief in the project and help collecting various pho-

tographs from the movie that appear in the book.

This book would not exist without the help of many enthusiastic and talented collaborators who are too numerous to mention. In particular, Erik Josowitz's creative and technical expertise brought this project to its fruition. For their editorial assistence I'd like to thank Bill Wise, Seth Maxwell, and Judy Montgomery. For her patience and fortitude in dealing with writers who apparently smoked pot all through high school English, my gratitude goes to our proofreader Kim Krizan. Anne Walker-McBay always lent an ear and created a wonderful working environment. And, of course, thanks to Richard Linklater whose initial vision made this project possible.

—Denise Montgomery,
Editor

ALRIGHT!
ALRIGHT!
ALRIGHT!

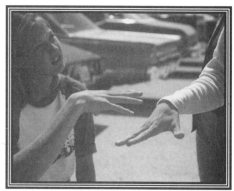

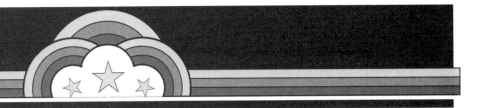

STILL DAZED
AFTER ALL THESE YEARS
BY RICHARD LINKLATER

About six years ago, I was driving along and heard an early ZZ Top song from their legendary "Fandango" album. I flashed to a 1976 night piled in a LeMans with three others, listening to the "Fandango" 8-track. I remembered how it clicked over from track to track all night long, and we drove around endlessly, looking for something to happen. A six-pack of beer, a joint, singing along with the music blasting out of the Craig Powerplays (or were those Jensen Tri-axels?), challenges from other cars, a brief flirtation with a car of girls, and the eventual regression into throwing garbage cans at mailboxes. At the end of the evening we had driven almost 150 miles and of course, had gotten nowhere. I don't think we'd even left the city limits of the suburban shit town we were stuck in. But from the perspective of a freshman in high school however, it seemed like great fun (especially a day, a month, or more than a decade later).

I knew I had a high school film to make and I also knew it could only be a bitter-sweet trip back. But, once committed, I felt I had no other choice but to jump in and embrace it all. I had to tap back into a period in my life I had long ago intentionally repressed. Even though I'd had what most would consider an okay enough high school "career," still it was all too painful. But contemplated from this safer distance, it all started to mean something more. I could trace the traits of my adult personality back to who I was at ages 14-17. Events and the atmosphere from a small East Texas high school I attended were my initial building blocks. I had also attended a large urban high school and drew on experiences and characters from there. I knew I couldn't encompass it all and only tried to concentrate on certain aspects. So many of the things in this movie never really happened of course, and none of the characters are based solely on one person I knew. But somehow it all feels true and accurate in a com-posite sort of way. I think it was part wish fulfillment, part revisiting old stupidities and pain. It was fun analyzing how an event or ritual would take on an almost metaphorical meaning to me or how people I had known many years ago seemed back in my life. I'd even have dreams at night where I was sitting with my high school newspaper staff discussing the movie.

It's always intrigued me the way the 70's appeared to be going down in history. When discussing that decade everyone seemed to be cynically concentrating on the kitchiest elements of the later 70's disco culture or some of the dumb hit songs throughout the decade. But hey, every time period has had it's short-lived fads and crazes and of course the best selling music, books, and movies most often don't stand the test of time. Always remember the top song of that "radical" year 1969 was by comic book characters (The Archies' "Sugar, Sugar"). So as always, a lot of goofy, mindless things were bought and sold in the 70's—so what else is new? But why was it that only this frothy perception of what the 70's were about got passed along as the official history? Was it an attempt to solidify the 60's (by comparison) as this ultimate in our cultural history by people who had obviously "peaked" and were content to nostalgically repeat it over and over for the rest of their lives (and ours)? I'm glad as teenagers we were aware that the time we were living in sucked—it's impossible to have much nostalgia for that time period. It's stupid to be nostalgic for any time period. If previous generations had been more aware, they would have realized that their teens sucked just as bad. Actually, probably worse. Let's face it, no matter where you live at no matter what time, High School is a light prison sentence to be served. Once paroled, you don't look back.

We grew up with the images of war, riots, assassinations not to mention that hovering dread that due to overpopulation, pollution, or nuclear bombs, there probably wouldn't be much of a world by the time we were old enough to enjoy it. American mid-to-late 70's society was probably a lot like the post-WWI 20's: after witnessing the horrors of war and realizing that humanity was capable of such large-scale corruption, destruction and loss, one might as well, as Jim Morrison said, "get your kicks before the whole shithouse goes up in flames." After such blood-lettings, maybe it's a part of the healing process to turn the attention away from the society that has let everyone down and to focus on where the party is. The 70's may have lacked the obvious singular political issues that had the ability to unite an entire culture (you or your friends getting shipped off to a possible death in a muddled war), but we did have the music and sometimes that seemed like enough to keep you going. Sure there was a lot of dreck, but the best of it has to constitute a classic era in rock history. Straightforward, honest—there is a certain timelessness to so much of it. You can't really get any more eternal than "You ain't seen nothin' 'till you're down on a muffin." This was music to have fun to, to crank up and to put the pedal to the metal to. It did what rock and roll was supposed to do—it unleashed a power and had a liberating and unifying affect.

What I'm really trying to say is you only go through high school and teenagerhood once, and for those of us who spent formative time in the 70's, it's all we've got in that category. All things considered, it seems we did okay. It's only now, as we get older, that we can begin to write our own history—the one we actually lived through. We didn't create our society or immediate environment—we only lived in it and got by as best we could. That's the plight of the teenager—trapped and oppressed, but with the budding consciousness of being trapped and oppressed, but still trapped and oppressed nonetheless. Hopefully you survive those years, get out

alive and start to maneuver through a bigger world where you can actually make a few choices for yourself (Careful—the new oppressors often seem friendly at first and sometimes even offer paychecks and benefits).

Many people have worked on this book. Once we had arrived at what this book would be—a kind of hybrid of a mid-70's high school yearbook, high school newspaper, and teen fanzine—I was basically finishing the movie while Denise Montgomery organized, conceptualized, and directed everybody along the way. It's been lots of fun reading what everyone has come up with and seeing how much fun they've had doing research, remembering old bits, and then writing from a teenager's perspective. This book has made little attempt to "summarize" the decade or make a lot of claims about it. Rather, like the movie, it is merely a snapshot from a teenage perspective, and a mostly teenage analysis, of a particular time in history. The time line runs from September 1973 through May of 1977 because those are the years the older characters in the movie are in high school. The younger characters would've run '76-'80 but that would have taken us in another direction altogether. I intentionally set the movie in the pre-disco, pre-punk era because, looking back, that bit of time seemed like the end of something—I'm not sure what. I just remember telling the entire cast that they were playing extraordinary people living in an unextraordinary place at an unextraordinary time. It was always a primary intention of the movie to show a continuum of teenage experience and how, in a way, very little has changed in the last seventeen years. Indeed, maybe teenagerland hasn't changed much at all in the forty years since the moment in Nicholas Ray's REBEL WITHOUT A CAUSE where Jim (James Dean) and Buzz (Corey Allen) stare over the edge of the cliff Buzz and his car are soon to accidentally plunge over in a game of "chicken":

Jim: Why do we do this?

Buzz: We gotta do something...

THE FRIENDLY FRATERNITY OF FREAKS

Doing Drugs In The Seventies

by Candi Strecker

Sixties people and Seventies people can't agree which era most deserves to be called "Drug Decade of the Century." Blame it on human nature: everybody wants to believe he or she grew up in the wildest, craziest, most exciting times that ever were. But to be fair, both decades have strong, but very different, claims to that coveted title. The Sixties can take credit for pioneering the mass use of recreational drugs, for shifting the national mood toward hedonism and taboo-smashing. But the Seventies may well be the druggiest of decades in terms of sheer numbers: that's when recreational drugs achieved market penetration. In those numbers, in those crowds pouring through the doors they'd opened, Sixties people got what they'd wished for, and weren't too happy about it. Many had sincerely believed in the liberating power of marijuana and LSD to bring about a "better world" once enough people had sampled them. That made sense back in the Sixties, when most people experimenting with drugs were clean, white, well-to-do college students, trust-fund kids, and Hollywood types. But how hip and clever could getting high be when teenagers, assembly-line workers and country-music listeners were all doing it? The Seventies fulfillment of the Sixties revolution was... unattractive blue-collar teens puking Quaaludes at a Grand Funk Railroad concert.

Even for those who lived through it, it's hard today to remember how drug-tolerant American culture was in the Seventies, how normal it was for people in all walks of life to have smoked a bit of marijuana or tried some illegal chemical. But the evidence is there, in the number of unblushing drug references in the decade's movies and TV shows, books and magazines, and pop song lyrics. By the strength of their numbers, drug users temporarily silenced their opponents. In that climate of permissiveness, even the straightest of parents and adults might have self-doubts: should we condemn something we've never tried ourselves? Is a joint that much worse than a martini? Drugs were illegal in theory but the law wasn't much of a deterrent. The police couldn't bust everybody, and with possession sentences being lowered to traffic-ticket levels in many places, going after discreet dope users wasn't worth the effort and paperwork. Everyone knew that full decriminalization of marijuana was just around the corner. Drugs in the Seventies were just illegal enough to make one feel a rush of rebellion and risk — all part of the fun.

Marijuana was the universal Seventies drug, the common denominator experience, the one illegal substance used by everybody who used anything. Smoking marijuana was the minimum requirement for membership in a subculture that was, in effect, the dominant culture of the Seventies youth generation. Once initiated into the friendly fraternity of dopers, one finally understood what all that wacky head shop paraphernalia was for: the incense and air-fresheners, the neatly pressed packets of rolling papers (Job, Rizla, Bambú, E-Z Wider), the laboratory-quality scales, the grow-your-own books, the racks of *High Times* magazine and underground comix, the baroque pipes and roach clips and tokers and bongs. (The quintessential Seventies sensory experience was the rank, penetrating morning-after smell of spilled bong-water on the shag carpet of a van.) It was a membership that could be worn, through marijuana-leaf jewelry or coke-spoon pendants or t-shirts with slogans like STONED AGAIN. Those worried about what mom would say preferred the ambiguous message of R. Crumb's KEEP ON TRUCKIN' t-shirts.

By joining the druggie fraternity one could share its secret language, which piggybacked double meanings onto stale old words. Parents and teachers were baffled by the giggling outbursts when they said the most ordinary words: rope. snow. trip. weed. head. More catch-phrases came from the drug-tinged comedy records by Cheech & Chong and The Firesign Theatre. And insiders recognized a whole category of Head Objects, innocent in themselves but wonderful enhancers of the stoned experience: black light posters, beanbag chairs, Pink Floyd's Dark Side of The Moon album, certain art books (Magritte, Dali, M.C. Escher), junk foods for the condition known as The Munchies. (Surely, Screaming Yellow Zonkers™ in the trippy Peter-Max-style box were deliberately targeted at the pothead market.)

Beyond marijuana, there was an ever-expanding menu of choices. Some liked "natural

drugs," a category that included hashish, peyote, mescaline and (illogically) LSD. Others preferred pills: Valium and other misused prescription uppers and downers, and the Seventies' hottest drug discovery, Quaaludes (sopors or soapers or 'ludes). Still others leaned toward pure chemicals: cocaine, speed, PCP (angel dust).

At its best, Seventies drug culture encouraged playfulness, experimentation, and curiosity. One example was the endless search for free or legal substances that would get one high. Some tried to read between the lines of Euell Gibbons' edible-weed books, others delved into old texts on botany and pharmacology, just in case some psychoactive plant had been overlooked. Recipes for preparing and ingesting morning-glory seeds, jimsonweed, nutmeg, banana peels, or mullein circulated by word-of-mouth. Little ads in head-shop magazines sold SAFE! LEGAL! HERBAL HIGHS by mail order: kava-kava root, yohimbe bark, wild lettuce. The wildly unreliable *Anarchist Cookbook* even claimed one could get a buzz from smoking dried toad skins. Nobody was ever that desperate for drugs, but many were bored and curious enough to try almost anything. Then there were the tantalizing rumors of pot growing wild in ditchrows, free for the gathering,

still seeding itself from the 1940's when farmers grew hemp as vital war material. Those who managed to find this "headache weed" learned that while it looked like the real thing, it usually failed the smoking test. Fragments of real-world technical knowledge could be channeled into various realms of dopery by those with time on their hands: marijuana brownie-baking, kitchen-sink chemistry, sensemilia botany with grow-lights and hydroponics, or the quest to engineer a better bong (or at least a cheaper one) from household objects like Pringles™ potato-chip cans.

Some of these activities were half-baked, others downright dangerous, but despite all the nonsense and sheer bullshit going around, skepticism had no place in the Seventies drug brotherhood. If you shouldn't trust anyone straight or over thirty, then you had a sacred obligation to believe anything said by any under-thirty freak! Similarly, enlightened consumers might demand organic vegetables and 100% cotton underwear but couldn't take that approach to drug buying. Unlike a Chiquita™ banana, marijuana didn't carry a coun-

try-of-origin sticker proclaiming it was truly Colombian, Panama Red, Acapulco Gold or Thai Stick. No Good Housekeeping Seal backed up the purity of one's purchase, which might be stretched with catnip or sugar or deliberately laced with paraquat, PCP or strychnine. Even with prescription drugs that could be looked up in the *Physician's Desk Reference*, most people passed up the chance to know what they were doing: hey, if it's a pill, I'll take it.

This kind of deliberately uninformed drug use was part of the Seventies generation's rite of passage: to dare their minds and bodies to deal with anything they could smoke, snort or swallow, without going insane or getting addicted or dying from some stupid risk taken while stoned. There was a certain contrary pride in taking and passing that test, the comradeship of soldiers who'd proved themselves under fire.

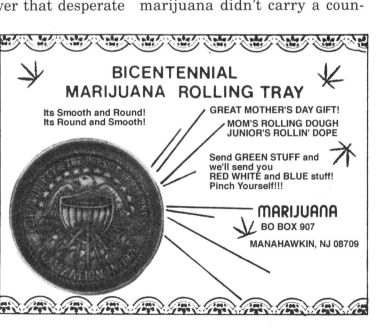

Any 8 records or

Music Club of America
NOW INVITES YOU TO TAKE . . .

SELECTION NUMBERS IN THE THOUSANDS ARE EITHER 2-RECORD SETS OR DOUBLE-LENGTH TAPES, AND COUNT AS TWO SELECTIONS—WRITE EACH NUMBER IN A SEPARATE BOX

Artist / Title	Number	LPs
TODD RUNGREN — Something Anything	0134	2 LPs
KRAFTWERK — Autobahn	0674	2 LPs
ROBIN TROWER — For Earth Below	0694	3 LPs
JEFF BECK — Blow by Blow	0434	2 LPs
CAPTAIN & TENNILLE — Love Will Keep us Together	0264	2 LPs
BARRY WHITE — Can't Get Enough	0792	2 LPs
AEROSMITH — Toys in The Attic	0344	2 LPs
HELEN REDDY — Free & Easy	1376	2 LPs
TONY ORLANDO&DAWN — Primetime	0546	2 LPs
ZZ TOP — Fandango	0295	2 LPs
OHIO PLAYERS — Fire	0721	2 LPs
STEVE MILLER — The Joker	0736	2 LPs
MOODY BLUES — This is the Moody Blues	0412	2 LPs
GRAND FUNK — Mar, Bon and Mell	0756	2 LPs
BILLY SWAN — I Can Help	0673	2 LPs
HUMBLE PIE — Street Rats	0941	2 LPs
MAC DAVIS — All the Love in the World	0679	2 LPs
CHUCK MANGIONE — Chase the Clouds Away	0567	2 LPs
TRAFFIC — Heavy Traffic	0695	2 LPs
JACKSON 5 — Dancing Machine	0971	2 LPs
PAUL ANKA — Feelings	0176	2 LPs
JIM CROCE — Photographs & Memories	0495	2 LPs
BARRY MANILOW — Mandy	0978	2 LPs
TOM T. HALL — Songs of Fox Hollow	0807	2 LPs
CAT STEVENS — Buddha and the Chocolate Box	0609	2 LPs
NEIL DIAMOND — Serenade	0709	2 LPs
O'JAYS — Survival	0394	2 LPs
CW MCALL — Black Bear Road	0978	2 LPs

Artist / Title	Number	LPs
THE SOUNDS OF LOVE — A To ZZZ	0594	2 LPs
LARRY CORYELL — Offering	0934	2 LPs
ELECTRIC LIGHT ORCHESTRA — Face The music	0224	2 LPs
CHICAGO VIII — Harry Truman	0604	2 LPs
CHUCK MANGIONE — Bellavia	0574	2 LPs
ROY CLARK — Greatest Hits	0396	2 LPs
FERRANTE & TEICHER — Spirit of 1976	0195	2 LPs
PHOEBE SNOW — Second Childhood	1835	2 LPs
WILLIE NELSON — Red Headed Stranger	1754	2 LPs
TOM JONES — Memories Don't Leave Like People	0354	2 LPs
BARBARA STREISAND — Lazy Afternoon	0454	2 LPs
MAC DAVIS — Baby Don't Get Hooked	0724	2 LPs
ARTHUR FIEDLER & THE BOSTON POPS	0675	2 LPs
BARRY MANILOW II — Mandy	0626	2 LPs
MAC DAVIS — Burnin' Thing	0172	2 LPs
FRANKIE VALLI — Close Up	0129	2 LPs
SONNY & CHER — Greatest Hits	0457	2 LPs

Artist / Title	Number	LPs
TELLY SAVALAS — Who Loves Ya Baby	0132	2 LPs
WAR — Why Can't We Be Friends	0623	2 LPs
THE CARPENTERS — Horizon	0665	3 LPs
STEVIE WONDER — Fulfillingness First Finale	0438	2 LPs
JANICE IAN — Aftertones	0264	2 LPs
MELISSA MANCHESTER — Better Days & Happy Endings	0734	2 LPs
SLY &THE FAMILY STONE — Greatest Hits	1523	2 LPs
OHIO PLAYERS — Pleasure	1365	2 LPs
YES — Close to the Edge	0349	2 LPs
STRAUSS — Also Sprach	0350	2 LPs
JIM CROCE — Life & Times	1412	2 LPs
STEPPENWOLF — 16 Greatest Hits	0719	2 LPs
STEVE MILLER BAND — Anthology	0678	2 LPs
JOAN BAEZ — Ballad Book	0926	2 LPs
CAT STEVENS — Matthew & Son	0919	2 LPs
NEW SEEKERS — Come Softly to Me	0617	2 LPs
JOHN COLTRANE — Best of Trane	0512	2 LPs
KRIS KRISTOFFERSON — Me and Bobby McGee	0313	2 LPs
STEREO TEST RECORD	0616	2 LPs
LYNN ANDERSON — I've Never Loved Anyone More	0301	2 LPs
HELEN REDDY — I Am Woman	0729	2 LPs
MANTOVANI — The Greatest Gift is Love	0907	2 LPs
MANTOVANI — All Time Romantic Hits	0702	2 LPs
DONALD BYRD — Places and Spaces	0602	2 LPs
PAUL SIMON — Still Crazy After All These Years	0914	2 LPs
RUFUS — featuring CHAKA KHAN	0893	2 LPs
RAY CONNIFF — I Write The Songs	0693	2 LPs
ART GARFUNKEL — Breakaway	0932	2 LPs

Artist / Title	Number	LPs
PERCY FAITH — Disco Party	0415	2 LPs
SWEET — Desolation Boulevard	0212	2 LPs
POINTER SISTERS — Steppin'	0816	3 LPs
LORETTA LYNN — Back to the Country	0395	2 LPs
BARRY MANILOW — Could it be Magic	0346	2 LPs
NANCY WILSON — The Best Of	0732	2 LPs
TAMMY WYNETTE — I Still Believe in Fairy Tales	0619	2 LPs
TANYA TUCKER — Greatest Hits	0114	2 LPs
AL GREEN — Greatest Hits	1144	2 LPs
FREDDY FENDER — Rock 'N Country	3455	2 LPs
BARBARA STREISAND — Classical Barbara	0714	2 LPs
GLENN CAMPBELL — Rhinestone Cowboy	0713	2 LPs
SLACKER FAMILY SINGERS — GREATEST HITS	0709	2 LPs
Paul Simon — There Goes Rhymin' Simon	0517	2 LPs
SANTANA — Greatest Hits	0312	2 LPs
DONNA SUMMER — Love to Love You Baby	0708	2 LPs
QUINCY JONES — Mellow Madness	0206	2 LPs
CHUCK MANGIONE — Land of Make-Believe	0541	2 LPs
LINDA RONDSTAT — Silk Purse	0695	2 LPs
OZEL — Allaturca	1546	2 LPs
NARVEL FELTS — Reconsider Me	1265	2 LPs
BILLY SWAN — Rock N' Roll Moon	0098	2 LPs
JIM NABORS — A Very Special Love Song	0461	2 LPs
CRYSTAL JADE — I Keep Comin' Back	0634	2 LPs
MELISSA MANCHESTER — Midnite Blue	0345	2 LPs
BARRY WHITE — Let The Music Play	0345	2 LPs
WATTSTAX	0976	6 LPs
NARARETH — Hair of the Dog	0456	2 LPs

tapes for only 99¢

plus shipping and handling

If you join now and agree to buy 6 more selections at regular Club Prices

GEORGE JONES — Memories Of Us	0135 — 2 LPs
GENE WATSON — Love in the Afternoon	0691 — 2 LPs
CONWAY TWITTY — Linda on My Mind	0614 — 3 LPs
FREDDIE HUBBARD — Liquid Love	0485 — 2 LPs
DIANA ROSS — As Mahogany	0863 — 2 LPs
ROGER WILLIAMS — I Honestly Love You	1262 — 2 LPs
PINK FLOYD — UMMA GUMMA	1313 — 2 LPs
BACHMAN TURNER OVERDRIVE — Head On	0798 — 2 LPs
ASLEEP AT THE WHEEL — Texas Gold	0682 — 2 LPs
HELEN REDDY — No Way To Treat A Lady	0919 — 2 LPs
BOBBY VINTON — Heart of Hearts	0826 — 2 LPs
BAY CITY ROLLERS — Saturday Night	0736 — 2 LPs
JANIS IAN — Between the Lines	0132 — 2 LPs
THE LETTERMEN — All Time Greatest Hits	0576 — 2 LPs
DONA FARGO — Whatever I Say Means I love	0653 — 2 LPs
KISS — Alive	0911 — 2 LPs
MITCH MILLER'S GREATEST SING ALONG	0679 — 2 LPs
GRAND FUNK RAILROAD — Caught in the Act	0567 — 2 LPs
TRAFFIC — Heavy Traffic	0665 — 2 LPs
EARTH, WIND & FIRE — Gratitude	0911 — 2 LPs
THE CJAYS — Keep on Keepin on	0576 — 2 LPs
THE OSMONDS — Crazy Horses	0385 — 2 LPs
HEAVY CREAM	0348 — 2 LPs
GILBERT O'SULLIVAN — Himself	0147 — 2 LPs
LAST TANGO IN PARIS	0819 — 2 LPs
PIPPIN — Original Cast	0278 — 2 LPs
MAMAS & PAPAS — 20 Golden Hits	0334 — 2 LPs
CASHMAN & WEST — A Song or Two	0936 — 2 LPs

FINALLY! A RECORD AND TAPE CLUB WITH NO "OBLIGATIONS"—JUST CHEAP MUSIC!

Simply mail the application below with your check or money order. Once we get your application, we'll put you on our mailing list for the Club's music magazine, which describes the ALBUM OF THE MONTH for each musical preference. . . plus hundreds of capsule reviews from every field of music. In addition, the magazine regularly offers BONUS SELECTIONS and TWOFERS, available to Club members only.

If you wish to receive the Selection n of the Month, do nothing and it will be express mailed directly to your doorstep. If you prefer an alternate selection or perhaps nothing at all, simply fill in the response card and promptly mail it within three weeks.

Your account will be activated and the selections you order will be mailed and billed at regular low, low, low Club prices. Currently, Club prices are $7.90 for records, $6.98 for reel tapes and cassettes.

(Double Selections may be somewhat higher).

After completing your agreement to buy 6 more selections within three years, you may cancel your enrollment or re-enroll for additional benefits.

NOTE: all applications are subject to authorization and Music Club of America reserves the right to reject any application

MUSIC CLUB OF AMERICA
CLUB HEADQUARTERS/ AUSTIN, TEXAS 78714

YES—I have enclosed a check or money order for $1.85, which includes 99¢ for 10 Stereo LPs, 10 8-track Cartridges, or 10 Tape Cassettes plus 86¢ for shipping and handling. Please rush me my Priority Membership Discount Card, my Music Club of America catalog, and my subscription to the monthly club magazine. If not completely satisfied, I may return the above ordered items within 14 business days for a full refund. I agree to abide by the terms outlined in this advertisement, and understand that I am obligated to purchase 6 more selections at regular club prices during the next two years.

Please RUSH me the following selections:

	❏ 8-Track Tape	❏ Tape Cassette	❏ LP Record
_____	❏ 8-Track Tape	❏ Tape Cassette	❏ LP Record
_____	❏ 8-Track Tape	❏ Tape Cassette	❏ LP Record
_____	❏ 8-Track Tape	❏ Tape Cassette	❏ LP Record
_____	❏ 8-Track Tape	❏ Tape Cassette	❏ LP Record
_____	❏ 8-Track Tape	❏ Tape Cassette	❏ LP Record
_____	❏ 8-Track Tape	❏ Tape Cassette	❏ LP Record
_____	❏ 8-Track Tape	❏ Tape Cassette	❏ LP Record

My main musical preference is (I am always free to choose from any catagory):
❏ Rock Folk ❏ ShowSoundtracks ❏ Blues/Jazz
❏ Classical ❏ Country/Western ❏ Teen Hits

❏ Mr.
❏ Mrs.
❏ Miss _____
Address_____
City _____
State_____ Zip Code_____
Do You Have A Telephone? (Check One) ❏ YES ❏ NO

CANADIANS: Mail to above address, orders will be handled by Music Club of North America. Prices and availability may vary slightly.

Skyrockets in Flight, Afternoon Delight!

by Seth Maxwell

It's the mid seventies. I'm being beat-up in the back of the school bus to the music of "More, More, More" by the Andrea True Connection that's blaring on the bus's AM radio. It segues* into "Couldn't get it Right" by the Climax Blues Band. The beating gets worse. I'm caught in a generation built on the ashes of the cultural revolution of the sixties, and I don't exactly feel "free as a bird, now."

From macramé to EST, the seventies put the sixties up for sale. Like a time-traveling monster, the music of the seventies reared its ugly head back in time, grabbing the whole generation of the sixties, scooping up the goodies, tagging it, labeling it, pricing it, and putting it up for sale in malls all across the country. It was the era of hard rock. A whole new generation had just arrived on the scene, eager for something. Something that could help them ignore the ongoing Vietnam war, the free love they missed in the sixties, the energy crisis, Watergate, and that there really wasn't anything better to do then to just kick back, light that doobie, and kick out the jams.

With a lot of the teen and the post-teen-scene being zoned out on pot and ludes most of the time, it was hard to find cultural heroes to look up to... but not that hard because the new cultural heroes were blasting out of the JBL's on your Pioneer stereo a far road from base-ball, hot-dogs, apple pie and Chevrolet. From the KISS

Army to Queen, a whole new set of monarchs was emerging, conquering the boundaries of "What do you want to be when you grow up?" Everybody wanted to be a Rock God. Nobody wanted to be president-what a bore!

Within the music culture of the seventies, there was a big difference in the types of music that were being put out over the air waves. That difference was quickly noticed by listening to what was being played on the AM and FM dials. AM was kid's stuff, while FM, (although a little more adult), was teen-scene a rama.

"Light Rock" was the standard for AM, playing songs like "Cats in the Cradle," to WAR's "Why Can't We be Friends." It was the stuff you listened to on your way to elementary school, featuring hit songs by artists you never heard of - like "Seasons in the Sun" by Terry Jacks, "Shannon," a song about some run away puppy dog ("Shannon has gone away, and drifted out to sea...") by Harry Gross, and "Afternoon Delight" by the Starland Vocal Band. It was a world of pseudo-psychedelia bubble gum. Although you probably had the 45's, you never bought the albums.

Now take that hit off your first joint... psssssssspt! Mornin' champ! Your 45's look like little Frisbees and your transistor radio doesn't look waterproof. Welcome to "high" school. Your graduation presents include a red portable AM/FM 8-track player, a three-foot bong, and Aerosmith's "Toys in the Attic." Abba doesn't sound as good after twenty bong-hits (although some people say they sound better...)

FM, Dolby stereo, and "Hard Rock" were the sounds that made Barry Manilow's beagle run into traffic with his tail between his legs. While Neil Sedaka was singing "Bad Blood," Gene Simmons drooled it. FM made radio more fun to listen to. Sure, your parents could put up with the

Carpenters "Close to You," but this was the stuff they really hated. Smoking a joint was like the background music for Led Zeppelin, Pink Floyd, Robin Trower, and Black Sabbath. You knew you were really stoned when you closed your eyes and saw Frampton come alive and understood every word Yes was saying.

The music included everyone. Not getting laid and missing all the free-love™ in the sixties was a big drag, but in the meantime, you could always fight to some good drinking music, or should I say drink to some good fighting music: Lynyrd Skynyrd, Black Oak Arkansas and Molly Hatchet — or you could "Mellow down easy" ala ZZ Top or the Allman Brothers.

The only thing better than FM was going to a live rock concert. They were the seventies' answer to sixties' be-ins. It was like a traveling Woodstock, more of an event than a show or a recital. It was something everybody looked forward to (along with hanging out with millions of people you've never met and partying each other's brains out). It didn't matter if you were cool or a total geek- everyone hung out together.

First scoring your tickets, then your weed, rock concerts were an excuse to get real fucked up. The smoke from the tons of weed being toked was enough to get anyone stoned. Your only worry was being searched and arrested for possession of marijuana or being busted a t the front door for sneaking in a bottle. It was always worth the risk. Safely inside, you could puke Boonesfarm to your heart's content. It wouldn't even matter who was on tour; Ted Nugent, Nazareth, Steve Miller or Bad Company, they were just the background music for the Bacchanalia inside the stadium.

With humongous stage shows duking it out for the largest arena attendance (or the tallest platforms), mega-rock shows like Cal Jam I or II, were a teenager's waste-land; it was way cooler than Disneyland. Who cared about the Matterhorn, when you could see the Abominable Snowman gutting and disemboweling people at an Alice Cooper Show. Treasure Island was completely for sissies when you could see Kiss live and the EPCOT Center was lame compared to Yes's round, revolving stage.

Concerts were a big juvenile delinquent playground for their stoned out inmates. With disco balls casting huge circles of light and spotlights sweeping over the audience, it was a blast. Blue Oyster Cult had some topless babe on the back of a Harley, as well as a giant Godzilla blowing fog from the side of the stage. I saw Alice Cooper rip off the heads of baby dolls and grab his victims right out of the audience. I still think it was staged.

Kiss had their risers for each band member which raised them miles above the stage making them great Frisbee targets, while Gene Simmons spat fire and drooled blood during "God of Thunder." They were one of the most intense bands to see live if you didn't lose your lunch. If you weren't too fucked up after the show, you could wander around the arena looking for left-over bags of weed, or the last swallow off a warm bottle of Southern Comfort (ugh, sometimes it's actually hard re-living these memories...). Anyway it was a lot more fun then watching them on TV.

This list of the triumphs and errors of the 70's could go on forever. Some people still curse the day it was hatched, cringing when they hear the first few notes to "Big ol' Jet Airliner." Whatever you think of the music of the seventies, as teenagers we embraced the music that surrounded us partly because we had no choice of when we were born. Of course everybody made the best of it, we still do. Mass gatherings at rock concerts always bring out a feeling of belonging through a sense of tribalism. For many of us the seventies provided a wide range of music that created a sense of balance which helped us to escape our middle class disillusionment and find our own nirvana. It allowed us to move ahead like a rolling stone crashing onto a stairway to heaven.

 "**Welcome to**

Who's Where? - Who's There?

① Commons Area (Cafeteria)
② Stoners
③ Motorheads
④ Jocks
⑤ Preps
⑥ Smoking Court
⑦ Dealer(s)
    a. Before School
    b. After School
    c. During lunch
⑧ Campus rent-a-cop

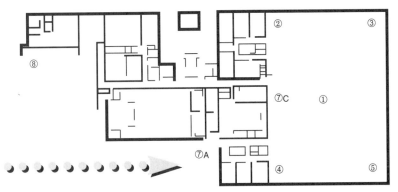

Rebel Country!"

. . . . when so many different lives happen together.

Todd Allen
Mary Blaise
Michelle Burroughs
Sheri Clester

Dan Coupland
Don Dawson
Debbie Dickinson
Cynthia Dunn

Kyle Eschenbrenner
Kaye Faulkner
Randall Floyd
Jodi Foreman

Madeline George
Keith Gilboy
Ellie Groskopf
Jodi Krammer

Simmone Kerr
Tina Lundquist
Darla Marks
Shirley Marsh

J. D. Martin
Mike Newhouse
Fred O'Bannion
Benny O'Donnell

Tony Olson
Chuck O'Toole
Kevin Pickford
Lester Riley

Irene Shingldecker
Kami Ridenour
Jimmie Sims
Julie Simms

Ron Slater
Melvin Spivey
Nesi White
Karen Wolfrat

Clark Wheeler
Shavonne Wright
Class Sponsors:
Coach Conrad
Ms. Stroud

17

Slater

Name: Ron Slater

Formative childhood experience: Telling his parents he's going on a day-long arrowhead hunt with friends, he attends a concert by ZZ Top and Santana at the state university's football stadium. A buxom woman wearing cutoffs and a t-shirt showing Richard Nixon feeling up the Statue of Liberty's says to Ron, "Wanna shotgun?" When he looks puzzled, grabs him behind the head and kisses him while vigorously blowing pot smoke into his lungs. Without consciously realizing it, Ron changes his life.

Role Models: The Fabulous Furry Freak Brothers

Early warning signs: As a boy, Ron spends hours gazing at the hallucinogenic panels drawn by Jack Kirby and Jim Steranko for various issues of Silver Surfer, Fantastic Four, and Nick Fury, Agent of Shield. Also sees 2001, a Space Odyssey nine times.

First flight: Two-thirds of the way through seemingly endless Jerry Garcia solo at a Dead concert, he is convinced he has levitated about two feet off the ground. Slater never quite comes down to earth again.

Wall posters: A silk-screened portrait of the bearded guy who appears on the cover of Zig Zag rolling papers, an enormous day-glo Hendrix, a picture from Rolling Stone of the Grateful Dead's Phil Lesh standing in front of a naked hippie chick, various concert posters, a *High Times* centerfold, and, over the bed, a life-sized nude of Jane Fonda sitting on a beach.

Bong ambition: Working on an anti-resin water pipe that merges NASA technology with ancient Asian hookah design; plans to approach Jimmy Page, Cheech and Chong, Robin Trower and other notable smokers for backing.

Utopian text: Charles Reich's The Greening of America, which he's been reading at the rate of several paragraphs a week for the past year or so. Also believes every word in Erich von Daniken's <u>Chariots of the Gods</u>.

Beacons of hope: Comet Kohutek, which is actually pretty awesome when enhanced by a telescope and mescaline, and the Viking I photos of Martian canals, which prove von Daniken was right.

Mystery chant: "Ahhhh fawa-kawa, pusseh pusseh," that inscrutable phrase John Lennon keeps repeating in "No. 9 Dream Song."

Pet conspiracy theory: Pot is illegal because William Randolph Hearst got together with the logging industry to keep cheap paper made from hemp off the market.

Slater's "101 WAYS TO SMOKE POT AT SCHOOL"

1. Always arrive early for school so you have more time to roll a good joint.

2. Leave all of your notebooks in the car so you can retrieve them one at a time. (This way you get to smoke before every class.)

3. Smoke underneath the hooded fans in the chemistry classroom.

4. Write yourself a doctor's excuse to get out of class/school, go anywhere, and toke yourself numb. Come back and tell them you're on heavy medication.

5. In the girls bathroom, take the top off of a tampon wrapper. Remove the tampon. Fill the empty hole with pot. Roll it up on both sides and flame it away. Smoke some cigarettes...

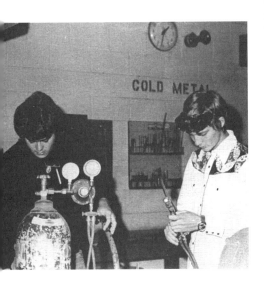

6. In metals/jewelry class you can always smoke in the room where you where you melt stuff (not to mention that you always have a flame handy).

7. Lunch break: anything goes.

8. Before school empty out half of a cigarette, load with weed and smoke during recess.

9. In between classes open your locker, light a Tokeless Pipe™, and exhale into the locker (or someone else's locker...)

10. When no ones in the science room, put some hash on pin, light, cover with a beaker and collect the smoke, lift, inhale. Later collect cool glass stuff to make bongs at home.

11. In the cafeteria, take some weed, put it on the food of your choice and munch out.

12. Take a photo-journalism class. This way you get the full "use" of the darkroom.

13. Keep failing drivers-Ed until you get an instructor who smokes pot. While practicing your skills, keep taking the wrong turns until you run out of gas. Light one up while you wait for a ride.

14. Smoke behind the kiln in ceramics class after firing up your new sculpture/bong.

15. Run to the school nurse, throw up and get sent home, load bong.

16. Light up underneath the bleachers at the football field. (WARNING: A lot of my friends have been busted here...)

17. Skip class and climb up to the catwalk in the auditorium and toke away the time. If you're lucky, you might get to see a play for free...(like my favorite high school plays, "Guys and Dolls" and "A Streetcar Named Desire").

18. In the automotive class, they let you test drive cars when you're done working on them. Drive off, light up, air out, and drive back.

continued page 116

19

Mike Newhouse

Early rebellion: Argues with the kiddy dentist about fluoride, which little Mike, parroting a magazine article he read at the barbershop, condemns as probably some sort of government plot.

Later rebellion: Argues with his eighth grade Social Studies teacher, Coach Judd, about the merits of the Vietnam War. They strongly disagree, and Mike is told to shut up and start obeying the school hair code.

Sophomore year frustration: Can't find any smart girls who like the same records he does except Cynthia Dunn, who, having gone through elementary school with him, is more like a sister.

Favorite albums: The Stones' *Exile On Main Street*, Roxy Music's *Siren* and Randy Newman's *Good Old Boys*, which causes big trouble when he plays it for Modern American History class, thanks to lines such as, "We're rednecks / We don't know our ass from a hole in the ground / And we're keeping the niggers down..."

Junior year frustration: Reads Thomas Pynchon's <u>Gravity's</u> <u>Rainbow</u>, understands about half of it, but can't find any teachers to discuss it with because none of them have finished reading the novel.

Favorite magazine: National Lampoon.

Money making brainstorm: Woody Allen lunchbox with scenes from "Love and Death" in episodic montage around the thermos.

Pet project: Currently writing teleplay entitled "Get Kristy McNichol." The star of Family would now be a private detective with cultural exchange student Nikita as scantily clad sidekick.

Pet Rock: Albert, as in Prince Albert. (Yes, he's kept in a can.)

Pet nightmare: To be stuck stage managing a touring company of "Godspell" forever. Three weeks into the production the actors decide to start performing naked. An entire wardrobe budget has been wasted on suspenders, rainbow wigs and smiley face buttons.

Pet peeve: The advent and the success of the iron-on transfer. In particular anyone wearing an "I'm with stupid" T-shirt.

Current anthem: Paul McCartney and Wings' "The Mess I'm In," a metal jackboot stomp inexplicably located on the B-side of the hit "My Love."

| END OF SCHOOL | # The Rebel Yell | FINAL ISSUE |

VOLUME 21 ISSUE 9   ROBERT E. LEE HIGH SCHOOL   MAY 16, 1976

What the Bicentennial means to Me.

by Simone Kerr
SPECIAL TO THE REBEL YELL

The bicentennial is a thing that only happens once in a life-time, and I guess that I happen to be lucky enough to live through it in my life-time...

I guess it's supposed to represent the 200 hundred years of freedom we've had here in the US. since the founding of this country in the first place... but for some reason, I kind of don't see the celebration as some thing our "fore-fathers" really had in mind.

For instance, do you really think George Washington would really be stoked on the idea that everything you buy this year is red, white, and blue? Like, come on, I guess this country was built around everybody making money off each other (capitalism), but red, white, and blue towels, mailboxes, fire hydrants, tacos, cars, houses, lunch boxes, clothes, jeans, guitars, dogs, cats... arrgh! Man! It's really driving me crazy, why are all these people cramming this stuff down my throat? I mean, O.K., I know Lincoln studied by candle light in his log cabin, and O.K., Ben Franklin discovered electricity with a kite and a key, but does that give anybody the right to make Log Cabin syrup, and Ben Franklin Savings and Loan?

I bet they wished that Ronald McDonald was a founding father—it would make everything much simpler going straight for the meat. Everything would be yellow, with red and white stripes, that way I could order a McPatriot made out of all-American beef.

And Hey, what's the idea of all this bicentennial money? Am I supposed to collect it or spend it?

Oh well at least my kids, if I live long enough to have any, won't have to deal with any of this stuff, but I'll really be glad when 1977 rolls around, 'cause hopefully something cool will happen. I mean, how much Barry Manilow can you listen to anyway?

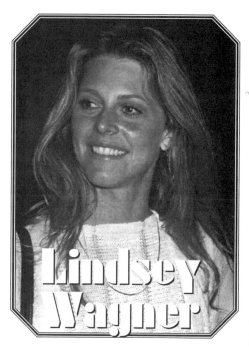

NAME: Lindsay Wagner

BIRTH DATE: June 22, 1949

BIRTH PLACE:
Hispanic slum in Los Angeles, CA

HAIR: Blonde

EYES: Hazel

SIGN: Cancer

TV CHARACTER:
School teacher Jaime Sommers aka
The Bionic Woman

FILM CREDITS: *Two People, Play Misty For Me, The Paper Chase, Second Wind*

**WHAT SHE WANTED
TO BE WHEN SHE GREW UP:**
A psychologist or a social worker

CHILDHOOD LIFE: Was always taking
care of children, including Glen Campbell's oldest daughter.

HOW SHE STARTED IN ACTING:
After failing at ballet and modern dance, she
began acting classes at age 14.

PAST LIVES: Became a Nina Blanchard model at
age 13, a career that lasted until she was 16;
later, a teacher for small kids,
a career that lasted five months.

SIGNS OF HUMAN FRAILTY:
Had ulcers when she was 14; got rid of
them by the time she was 21.

SCHOOLING:
University of Oregon (two semesters)

**HER BIG BREAK INTO
SHOW BUSINESS:** Meeting Lane Allen, the casting director for Marcus Welby, led her to a contract with Universal in 1971.

**CHALLENGES OF BEING
*THE BIONIC WOMAN:*** Historically a non-ath-
lete, she has to do a lot of her own stunts; doesn't
get to sleep as late as she used to.

**MESSAGE SHE'S TRYING
TO COMMUNICATE THROUGH
*THE BIONIC WOMAN:*** Things that
are important for kids to know.

FAVORITE RECIPES: Roquefort dressing

PAST BEAU: Estranged hubby Allan Rider

FAVORITE BEAU: Michael Brandon, formerly
Kim Novak's one and only.

PROBLEM WITH FAME: She can't go to a
McDonald's and buy a Big Mac.

22

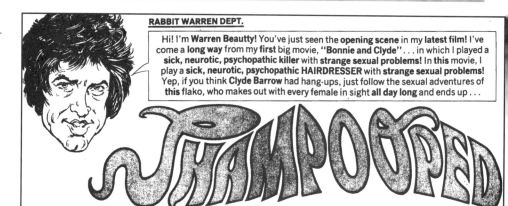

RABBIT WARREN DEPT.

Hi! I'm **Warren Beautty!** You've just seen the **opening scene** in my **latest film!** I've
come a **long way** from my **first** big movie, **"Bonnie and Clyde"** . . . in which I played a
sick, neurotic, psychopathic killer with **strange sexual problems!** In this movie, I
play a **sick, neurotic, psychopathic HAIRDRESSER** with **strange sexual problems!**
Yep, if you think **Clyde Barrow** had hang-ups, just follow the sexual adventures of
this flako, who makes out with every female in sight **all day long** and ends up . . .

SHAMPOOPED

the boogie van

MAKE:
1972 Ford Econoline Van.

DRIVEN BY:
Slater; when he's lucky enough to borrow it from his Uncle Bob.

ENGINE:
351 with an Edelbrock manifold 700cfm, Holley four-barrel, Heddman Hedders.

WHEELS:
Cragar SS with 127" wheelbase.

C.B. RADIO:
23 channel Boman-Astrosonix CB 720.

FRONT SEATS:
Hi-Rider™XL-75, 360° swivel bucket seats.

RADIO:
Muntz eight-track tape player and AM/FM tuner with Jil™ quad sound system.

FRONT SEATS:
Bise™ high back swivel buckets.

8-TRACK TAPES:
(Uncle Bob's stash): "This is the Moody Blues", Paul McCartney's "Band on the Run", Barry White's "Greatest Hits."

ADD ONS:
3 foot side pipes, air foil over rear door.

INTERIOR FEATURES:
A full wet bar, T.V., convertable couch to double bed, a 5-gallon aquarium. Cherry red crushed velvet upholstery and curtains. Black high-low shag carpet.

COLOR:
Fire engine red.

CUSTOM LETTERING:
Pearl yellow.

BUMPER STICKER:
"Onward through the fog."

Cynthia Dunn

Formative experience: Cynthia sees her first Bob Dylan show from the vantage of her mother's knee when she is four years old.

Heroines: Amelia Earhart, Gloria Steinem, and the courageous war correspondent and former Hemingway spouse Martha Gellhorn.

Adolescent Bible: <u>Diaries of Che Guevara</u>, whom she considers the sexiest man in history, along with Bobby Kennedy.

Favorite movie: *Chinatown*. Her parents applaud it as a dark parable of capitalism but she secretly loves it because Jack Nicholson's weary wiseass quality is somehow even more exciting than Che's burning nobility.

Strange feelings: Unimpressed by stories of promiscuity that, if true, would rank her high school alongside Caligula's Rome, she is moved to genuine curiosity by Nicholson's postcoital scene with Faye Dunaway. A born researcher, she scours her parents' massive library, turning up the Chinese classic A Carnal Prayer Mat, Anais Nin's <u>Delta of Venus</u>, the Kama Sutra, <u>Fanny Hill</u>, and to her surprise, Jacqueline Susann's <u>Valley of the Dolls.</u> She uses her newfound knowledge of fetishes and kinks to shock loudmouthed peers at school.

Sex: High school boys are either morons or klutzes. Decides to wait.

Favorite records: Todd Rundgren's *Something/Anything*, and David Bowie's *Ziggy Stardust and the Spiders From Mars*, which convinces her all the Black Sabbath fans at school must have terminal brain damage.

Favorite leading lady: Diane Keaton; she still exudes a genuine vulnerable sexuality even when resorting to "Woody Allen" simpering.

Recent accomplishment: Writing a monthly movie column for the Rebel Yell.

Home perm manufacturer: Toni™.

Brady buddy: Jan, the misunderstood middle sister. She got the brains, the braces, the glasses, the acne and the gurgling little sister.

Dream job: Film critic or television news producer like Mary Richards on the *Mary Tyler Moore* show, but with more radical content.

Ambitions: Attend Vassar, lose virginity, live in Europe, and write a novel.

PROFILES in CONFUSION

J A W E D

| Rebels Rule OK | The Rebel Yell | High and Mild |

The Rebel Yell

VOLUME 21 ISSUE 9   **ROBERT E. LEE HIGH SCHOOL**   September 8, 1975

DUBIOUS DISASTER FILMS

BY CYNTHIA DUNN

From the cafeteria, to the gym, to home room, to the lockers. All everyone seems to talk about these days is JAWS — the new movie that opened over our summer vacation. If you haven't seen it yet, it's about a 25 ft.+ great white shark that terrorizes a small resort town on the East Coast, and stars Richard Dreyfuss (from AMERICAN GRAFFITI) as a marine biologist, and Roy Scheider as the town's police chief. I will admit that it's very frightening, and had me on the edge of my seat biting my nails the entire time (as I'm sure it did for a lot of other people who have seen it). But, what really makes me cringe is when I hear some members of our student body refer to this excellent film as just another one of those "disaster movies," such as AIRPORT, AIRPORT '75, THE POSEIDON ADVENTURE, EARTHQUAKE, and THE TOWERING INFERNO. As "disaster movies" go, there is nothing remotely entertaining about lives lost and countless injuries suffered from a plane crash, or from a capsized ship, from a deadly California earthquake, or from a high-rise building engulfed in flames. Hollywood exploits these potential real-life tragedies by using them as a backdrop for slap-dash, badly acted soap operas (which you can watch on TV on any weekday afternoon without leaving your house) for Hollywood Has-Beens and Never-Weres to star in. And to really lure you into the theater, sometimes they come up with some stupid gimmick — like sensurround — which was used in EARTHQUAKE. This was supposed to make the audience experience what "real" earthquake tremors should feel like. Actually, it felt more like I was parked next to Kevin Pickford's car in the student parking lot with the bass on his stereo cranked up full blast than in an "actual" earthquake (although Ron Slater said that sensurround "freaked him out so bad" that he threw up in the second row of the theater — but then again, he's just kind of strange anyway). So, fellow students, JAWS is not just another stupid "disaster movie" (a trend, I hope, that we've finally seen run its course). It is a horror story drawn from the age-old struggle of man versus nature — and there's nothing fishy about that.

KISS Mania Grabs High School In Cadillac, Michigan

CADILLAC— It looked like a scene from a science-fiction movie at the Cadillac High School homecoming bonfire last night: hundreds of young faces painted up like worshippers of some alien race about to descend in their midst. But it was just part of the KISS mania that rocked and rolled into town earlier in the day.

Towering in platform boots and wearing second skins of black leather, the four members of the heavy metal rock band KISS arrived at the high school in the afternoon to a tumultuous welcome from students massed on the lawn. Wading through the students, the paint-masked rock stars entered the gymnasium for more photos and then were escorted to a classroom to view a film, made by several members of the football team, that mimed the KISS show.

The next stop was the band rehearsal room for questions from the players and cheerleaders, as photographers continued snapping away. Then on to the football field for more photos with the team and the marching band, which had learned several KISS tunes for the occasion.

Through all this, a small sea of whitened faces with black eyes followed the group as closely as possible; reporters and photographers squeezed through the crowd.

Evening festivities began with the bonfire, though no one would light it until Gene Simmons, KISS bass player, showed up to display his fire-breathing talent. Then it was time to burn the effigy of a Chippewa Hills Warrior and head for the gym and the main event: KISS in concert.

The crowd moved steadily in, the faces of parents standing out for their lack of decoration. Sound and lighting equipment filled the stage and to either side

K I  S S

of it stood more speakers. The students greeted the warm up band Double Yellow Line with mixed reactions, a few yelling for KISS to come out. But they soon got in the mood when the band played several hard rockers.

During the break between acts, the crowd stretched in what little room they had, the tension mounting steadily. Once the equipment for KISS was set, the audience began shouting and clapping with every check of the lights or movement of a stagehand.

Suddenly the lights went out, and it was time. KISS popped onto the stage and a roar went up from blackened lips. Giving their blessing to Cadillac and the Vikings. KISS started pounding out their hits. It was a fast-paced show — there were flames, flashes and smoke to go with the colored lighting. The din was incredible as wild cheering mixed with raucous guitars and drums. There was a short break as KISS and representatives of the school exchanged commemorative plaques. After several brief retreats from stage near the end of the show, KISS came back to do the song students and teachers had been chanting all day, "I want to rock and roll all night, and party every day." As the gym filled with the chorus, foam snow came billowing down from above the band.

While the final chords were still echoing loudly in everyone's ears, KISS was gone and the lights came up to reveal a tired and somewhat dazed audience. There was still school today to get some sleep for, though, for many, the excitement probably made it difficult.

"For years we have been trying to unite the student body and faculty. KISS accomplished this in one night," quoted from Cadillac Principal John Laurent at a press brunch earlier honoring the group where they were also presented with the key to the City from the Honorable Raymond Wagner (Mayor of Cadillac, Michigan) and his lovely wife. Also in attendance were Donald Mason, City Manager, William Smith, Superintendent of Schools, Dave Brines, Cadillac High School Football Coach, and Jim Neff, Assistant Football Coach. All were in full KISS make-up when KISS presented the above officials engraved plaques making them honorable KISS members.

Today, the band was expected to participate in the homecoming parade before departing Cadillac for the rest of their national tour. But they won't soon be forgotten by CHS and the students that wildly welcomed them to Cadillac.

Reprinted from the Cadillac Evening News.

ARMY

"GET A HAIRCUT!"

HELPFUL HINTS FROM SHAUONNE:
Ten ways to open a beer without a bottle opener

1. Bic lighters
2. keys
3. screwdrivers
4. place top edge on counter and slam down with fist
5. slowly maneuver a 2000 pound churchkey (the door of your car)
6. pliers
7. drill into the bottle-cap and use a straw
8. belt buckles
9. use your teeth
10. get cans

Shavonne Wright

Current crushes: Keith Carradine and Jackson Browne.

Success secrets: Continually amused at the deranging effect she has on boys. Her parents taught her that: "Anything worth doing is worth doing Wright," so she memorizes <u>The Joy of Sex</u>.

Favorite song: "When the Levee Breaks" by Led Zeppelin.

Memorable high school party: The 1974 Halloween Dance, dressed as Faye Dunaway in *Bonnie & Clyde*, she causes a sensation and meets Don Dawson. They begin a passionate, on-again-off-again romance as the band cranks out the Eagles' "Already Gone."

High school diversion: Going to the beach with friends, where they take mescaline, recline on beach furniture, and watch imaginary sunsets.

Cigarette brand: LemonTwists™ Menthol 100s.

Favorite woman TV. cop: Pepper on Police Woman.

Worst rumor: "The padding predicament," as it was later called. "Not only are they hers," contested an angry Don Dawson, "But I'm poundin' the dude that started this crap." Inside sources revealed, as did Shavonne, that everything was legit and in working order. This revelation, however, started a second nasty episode affectionately referred to as "the slut situation."

Secret pet name: Darla dubs her "Sparkle" after a drunken Shavonne continues to sing the chorus of Seals and Krofft's "Diamond Girl" during a much needed nature break at their first beer bust.

Ambition: Movie stardom before she is 25.

Home drinking tip: Remember to adjust the pencil lines on the liquor bottles at parent's wet bar. Iced tea is a great bourbon "equalizer."

BASIC TRADE AND INDUSTRIAL EDUCATION
When a bong goes wrong...

Ron Slater on the unsung craft of waterpipe maintenance.

Kyle: Man... I'm losing pressure...
I knew I should have made an owl cutting board.
Slater: No, Grasshopper, you must believe,
make the dream a reality.

MELBA

TOAST!

MAKE: Wooderson "Melba Toast"
1970 Chevrolet Chevelle SS
DRIVEN BY: Wooderson
ACQUIRED BY: Wooderson's earnings from a college football scholarship he drops, opting for Jr. college and the car
ENGINE: Big Block 454 w/cowl induction system
HORSEPOWER: 360c 4,440 rpm
TORQUE MAX.: 500 ft/lbs. c 3200 rpm

8-TRACK: Craig™ Powerplay with a 40 watt output
TAPES: Pink Floyd, Led Zeppelin, Bad Company, Lynyrd Skynyrd
BORE AND STROKE: 4.25 X 4
TRUNK CAPACITY: 2 people with room to roll or 5 people sneaking into drive-in movie
AFTERMARKET EXTRAS: Holly 750 cfm Double pumper, Edelbrock intake, 11.5:1 pop-up pistons, 4:11 positrac rear end

TRANSMISSION: 4/5 spd. Muncie M-ZZ "Rock Crusher"
LAST TICKET RECEIVED: For "open headers" by Officer Bozzio
GLOVE BOX CONTENTS: A big pocket comb, spark plugs, condoms, carburetor manual
BUMPER STICKER: "Gas, Grass, or Ass: Nobody Rides for Free"
HANGING FROM REAR-VIEW MIRROR: Garter belt from "Yellow Rose"

Kyle: Now I'll never get high.
Slater: A rubber washer at the base of the bowl is all you need circus pal—relax. If you're in a time crunch, wad up some *Bazooka Joe* and you're set.

Kyle: Gee Slater man, thanks alot.
Slater: Sure dude.
Kyle: What would I do you without you?
Slater: Same thing, just alone...

29

RICK WAKEMAN (YES)

creem
1975 reader's POLL

THE WHO

BRUCE SPRINGSTEEN

TOP TWENTY GROUPS

1. Rolling Stones
2. Led Zeppelin
3. The Who
4. Aerosmith
5. Kiss
6. Bad Company
7. Roxy Music
8. Queen
9. Elton John
10. Pink Floyd
11. Bruce Springsteen
    & the E Street Band
12. Black Sabbath
13. Rod Stewart
    & the Faces
14. David Bowie
15. Eagles
16. Sparks
17. Jefferson Starship
18. The Tubes
19. Alice Cooper
20. Yes

TOP TWENTY ALBUMS

1. Physical Graffiti (Led Zeppelin)
2. Born to Run (Bruce Springsteen)
3. Toys in the Attic (Aerosmith)
4. Young Americans (David Bowie)
5. Kiss Alive
6. Captain Fantastic and the
   Brown Dirt Cowboy (Elton John)
7. The Who By Numbers
8. Rock of the Westies
   (Elton John)
9. Wish You Were Here (Pink Floyd)
10. Sabotage (Black Sabbath)
11. Atlantic Crossing (Rod Stewart)
12. Red Octopus (Jefferson Starship)
13. Welcome to My Nightmare
    (Alice Cooper)
14. Blow By Blow (Jeff Beck)
15. Venus & Mars Are Alright Tonight
    (Paul McCartney & Wings)
16. Made In the Shade
    (Rolling Stones)
17. Frampton (Peter Frampton)
18. Ian Hunter
19. The Tubes
20. Dressed to Kill (Kiss)

TOP TEN SINGLES

1. Fame (David Bowie)
2. Born to Run (Bruce Springsteen)
3. Miracles (Jefferson Starship)
4. Ballroom Blitz (Sweet)
5. One of These Nights (Eagles)
6. Sweet Emotion (Aerosmith)
7. Young Americans (David Bowie)
8. I'm Not In Love (10cc)
9. Tush (Z.Z. Top)
10. Rock 'n' Roll All Night (Kiss)

TOP TEN R&B SINGLES

1. Fame (David Bowie)
2. Get Down Tonight
   (K.C. & The Sunshine Band)
3. Shame, Shame, Shame
   (Shirley & Company)
4. Lady Marmalade (Labelle)
5. Games People Play (Spinners)
6. Shinin' Star (Earth, Wind & Fire)
7. Cut the Cake
   (Average White Band)
8. The Hustle (Van McCoy)
9. That's the Way
   (K.C. & the Sunshine Band)
10. Jive Talkin' (BeeGees)

ROBERT PLANT

ALICE COOPER

N.O. I'M NOT EDDIE HASKELL

"A lot more time to listen to music because nobody had jobs."
John DePaul, Erie, PA

Reprinted from *Creem Magazine.*

ZZ TOP

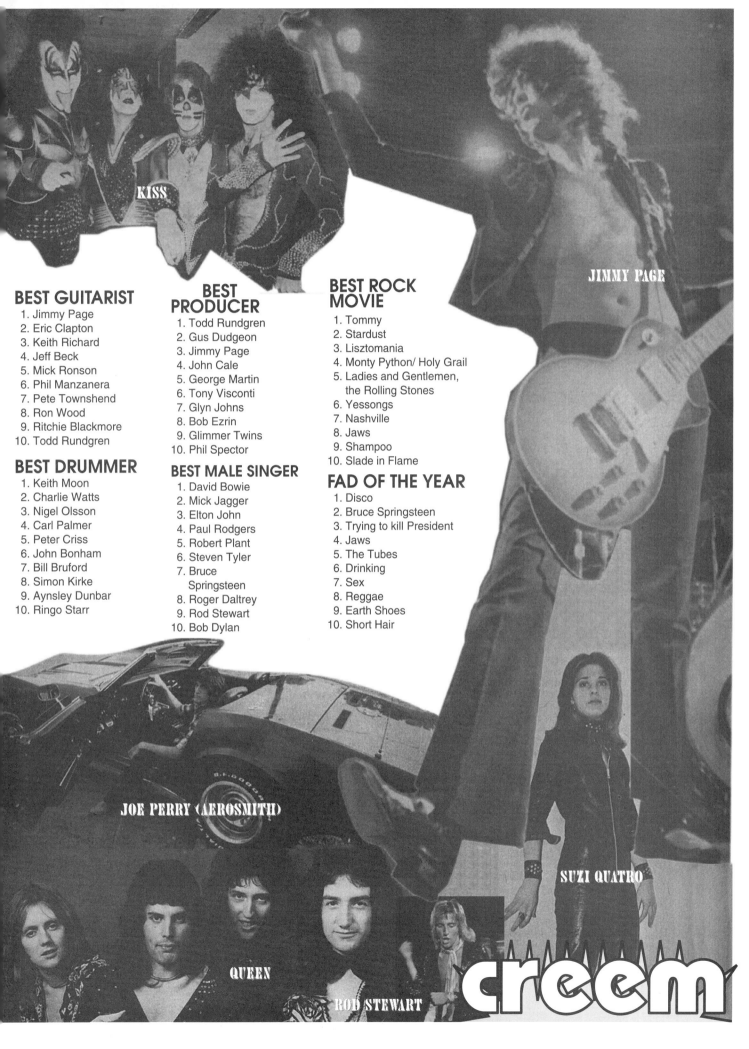

KISS

JIMMY PAGE

BEST GUITARIST
1. Jimmy Page
2. Eric Clapton
3. Keith Richard
4. Jeff Beck
5. Mick Ronson
6. Phil Manzanera
7. Pete Townshend
8. Ron Wood
9. Ritchie Blackmore
10. Todd Rundgren

BEST DRUMMER
1. Keith Moon
2. Charlie Watts
3. Nigel Olsson
4. Carl Palmer
5. Peter Criss
6. John Bonham
7. Bill Bruford
8. Simon Kirke
9. Aynsley Dunbar
10. Ringo Starr

BEST PRODUCER
1. Todd Rundgren
2. Gus Dudgeon
3. Jimmy Page
4. John Cale
5. George Martin
6. Tony Visconti
7. Glyn Johns
8. Bob Ezrin
9. Glimmer Twins
10. Phil Spector

BEST MALE SINGER
1. David Bowie
2. Mick Jagger
3. Elton John
4. Paul Rodgers
5. Robert Plant
6. Steven Tyler
7. Bruce Springsteen
8. Roger Daltrey
9. Rod Stewart
10. Bob Dylan

BEST ROCK MOVIE
1. Tommy
2. Stardust
3. Lisztomania
4. Monty Python/ Holy Grail
5. Ladies and Gentlemen, the Rolling Stones
6. Yessongs
7. Nashville
8. Jaws
9. Shampoo
10. Slade in Flame

FAD OF THE YEAR
1. Disco
2. Bruce Springsteen
3. Trying to kill President
4. Jaws
5. The Tubes
6. Drinking
7. Sex
8. Reggae
9. Earth Shoes
10. Short Hair

JOE PERRY (AEROSMITH)

SUZI QUATRO

QUEEN

ROD STEWART

creem

NAME: John Travolta
BIRTH DATE: February 18, 1954
BIRTH PLACE:
Englewood, New Jersey
HAIR: Brown
EYES: Blue
SIGN: Aquarius
HERITAGE: Irish-Italian
TV CHARACTER:
Vinnie Barbarino on
"Welcome Back Kotter"
FIRST FILM: *The Devil's Rain*

HOW HE BROKE INTO
SHOWBIZ: Dropped out of high
school at age 16 to do summer
stock in New Jersey and
eventually got some off-
Broadway parts.
RISE TO FAME: Moved to
Hollywood, joined the national
touring company of "Grease,"
and appeared in "Over Here"
with the Andrews Sisters.

WHAT'S NEW: A singing
career: At a recent record
release appearance in Hicksville,
New York, his adoring fans
started a full-fledged riot and
he had to escape disguised as
a policeman.
LATEST PLAYTHING: Diana
Hyland, who he met while film-
ing the TV movie, "Boy in a
Plastic Bubble."

Word Search Puzzle

```
R  E  T  Y  L  L  O  D  U  O  T  S
A  I  N  A  M  A  O  E  N  F  A  Y
G  R  C  O  R  N  E  L  I  U  S  A
O  U  I  S  N  O  A  I  V  N  F  K
L  N  S  I  A  O  R  E  R  K  R  I
D  A  E  S  I  N  G  L  A  A  A  R
E  W  V  U  M  R  A  I  M  I  M  S
N  A  E  F  E  E  S  E  A  K  P  C
O  Y  N  U  H  T  M  G  R  I  T  H
M  S  M  R  O  F  T  A  L  P  O  N
I  T  S  E  B  A  S  T  I  A  N  E
S  T  Y  U  H  P  W  O  N  D  E  R
```

20. FUNK
19. DONNIE
18. MANIA
17. SEVEN
16. DOLLY
15. MARVIN
14. WONDER
13. MARIE
12. PLATFORMS
11. EARGASM
10. BOHEMIAN
9. CORNELIUS
8. KIRSCHNER
7. RUFUS
6. SIMON
5. FRAMPTON
4. SEBASTIAN
3. RUNAWAYS
2. GOLDEN
1. AFTERNOON

Within this puzzle, you'll find at least 20 words associated with music in 1976, however loosely. How many can you find by consulting the brief clues? The names read forward, backward, up, down, or diagonally. We've started you off by circling AFTERNOON, the answer to number 1 in the diagram. The names may overlap and letters may be used more than once, but not all of the letters will be used.

1. When Starland-ers get it.
2. Bowie's years.
3. "Minor" gals' rock group.
4. "Welcome Back"'s John.
5. Do you feel like he do?
6. Crazy Paul, after all this time.
7. Featuring Chaka Khan.
8. "Rock Concert" Promoter.
9. M.C. on "Soul Train."
10. Queen's Rhapsody.
11. Johnnie Taylor's Disco Lady LP.

12. Dangerous shoe trend.
13. She's a little bit country.
14. Motown's $13 million deal.
15. I want you Gaye.
16. A voice you could bring home to mama.
17. How many words on Carlin's bleep list?
18. Bay City Roller _____.
19. He's a "little" bit rock-n-roll.
20. Grand____Railroad

EVENING

6:00 **2** (7) **News**
5 **Bewitched**
(9) **It Takes a Thief**
6:30 **11** Star Trek
5 **The Partridge Family**
13 **The Electric Company**
(7) **Voyage to the Bottom of the Sea**
7:00 **2** **News: Walter Cronkite**
4 **News: John Chancellor**
5 **Andy Griffith**
(7) **News: Harry Reasoner**
(9) **Ironside**
11 **Dick Van Dyke Show**
7:30 **2** **The 20,000 Pyramid**
4 **Don Adams Screen**
Test: Bob Newhart, Shirely Jones, guest (R)
5 **Adam 12**
(7) **Let's make a Deal**
11 **Family Affair**
8:00 **2** **Movie: "Skin Game"**
(1971). James Garner
4 **Sanford and Son (R)**
5 **The Crosswits**
(7) **Donny and Marie:**
Charo, The Osmond Brother's, George Gobel, Roy Clark, guests (R)
8:30 **4** **The Practice**
5 **Merv Griffin Show**
9:00 **4** **Rockford Files (R)**

(7) **Movie: The Burglers(1972).** Jean-Paul Belmondo, Omar Sharrif, Dyan Cannon
11 **Bonanza**
10:00 **2** **CBS Reports**
4 **Police Story**
5 **11** **News**
11:00 **2** **4** 7 **News**
5 **Mary Hartman, Mary Hartman**
(9) **The Lucy Show**
11 **The Honeymooners**
11:30 **2** **Movie: "Smash-up Alley"**
(1973). Darren McGavin, Noah Beery Jr.
4 **The Tonight Show**
5 **Movie: "Only Angles Have Wings" (1939).** Cary Grant, Rita Hayworth
(7) **The Rookies**
(9) **Movie: "Husbands" (1970)** John Cassavettes, Ben Gazzara, Peter Falk

EARLY SATURDAY

Mid. **11** **Movie: "Love Happy"**
(1950). The Marx Brothers, Marilyn Monroe.
12:30 (7) **Movie: "It! The Terror From Beyond Space" (1958).** Marshall Tompson
1AM **4** **The Midnight Special**

Benny O'Donnell

Formative childhood experience:
After committing two errors in a little league game, his irate father/coach had three of his teammates line up and simultaneously throw baseballs at him (Benny's strategy: catch one, dodge two.)

Only movie admits crying to:
"Brian's Song."

Thwarted ambition:
Thought about playing guitar but got frustrated after spending three hours trying to learn "Smoke on the Water" by Deep Purple.

Football hero:
Dick Butkus.

Baseball hero:
Harmon Killebrew.

Basketball hero:
Bill Russell.

Race car driver:
Richard Petty.

Favorite beer:
Schlitz, but will make do with his father's brand, Pabst Blue Ribbon.

Beer limit:
Once drank a case-and-a-half and made it home with only minor damage to his car's clutch.

Favorite albums:
ZZ Top's "Tres Hombres," Allman Brothers' "Eat a Peach."

New C.B. handle:
Ben Dover (formerly "The Sailing Rabbit")

On hold:
Refuses to smoke pot until it's legal.

Immediate aspiration:
To secretly get better at foosball, to get even larger and win state next fall.

Farther down the line:
A football scholarship and the long-awaited line of women outside his dorm door.

Favorite football chant:
"We ain't here to make friends; we're here to kick some ass."

Benny O'Donnell
English 12
2nd Period
Miss Dore *date?*

Writing Assignment: Why art appreciation is important to good citizenship.

Title: I Wanna Rock and Roll All Night and Party Everyday.

You need better evidence

A brief survey of my friends and their social activities last weekend shows that art appreciation is important to good citizenship. *Style too casual* Grant will tell you that Led Zepplin is the most important band in history. Grant is very tall and drinks beer faster than *inappropriate* anyone I know, so he has a lot of credibility. You might think *Keep in the third person.* that Zep are a bunch of English freaks *slang* but you better not say that in front of Grant. Billy, however, feels strongly that Lynard Skynard *Who?* are Gods. Stupid, but that is his constitutional right. *sentence fragment* I would argue that the music of Aerosmith has the most positive influence on today's youth. *Why?* Except "Dream on." *another sentence frag.* Which sucked *rude, inappropriate* "Combination" is definately their coolest song. Steve, poor Steve, is a raving fanatic for Kiss. This of course makes him the object *Not self-evident!* of continual abuse. My little sister is even to mature to like Kiss. There're *They're* not even real musicians. But this is a free country and as citizens of the U.S.A. we can choose our own role models. *Expand theme of democracy* *What does maturity have to do with it?* *What does this have to do with citizenship?*

The artistic influence of Gene Simmons on Steve shows how good citizen ship is caused by art appreciation. *Good reference to thesis (although thesis a bit weak)* Steve is fucking *insulting* allways, sticking out his tongue because he thinks it looks just like his hero's. He also is known to suddenly take off his pants in public and is often seen urinating is *in* crowded places. *Good citizenship?*

Last Friday, as a good citizen project, Steve talked us into dressing up like Kiss before we went out for the night. At first

choose more specific adjectives

inappropriate

I thought the idea ~~was faggoty.~~ But we actually looked ~~fucking~~
cool. I was Ace and ~~of course~~ Steve was Gene.

nice detail

So we piled into   GTO, cranked "Detroit Rock City" on the
Craig Power Play and took off for Forest Lane. At McDonald's

stolen?

we decided that the GTO needed some costume work too so we duct-
taped a big plastic trash can top (with the swinging door that
said "push" on the front) to the hood of the car to make a cool
hood scoop. Boss. We cranked the stereo (going) "I wanna rock
and roll all night and party every day."

Let's have a parent-teacher conference about this drinking

So we're driving around getting totally wasted on Michelobs
and at every red light we pile out doing monster air guitar and
throwing empties at street signs. Kiss "Alive" is blasting"
how many of you people out there like to drink cold gin?

I hope this is fictional.

Steve is standing on the hood with the (cool) McDonald's hood
scoop while we're cruising down Forest Lane. He's got his pants
completely off, playing bass on a Michelob bottle, singing,
"I'm the King of the Night Time World and You're My Headlight Queen."
We all run into the bowling alley, full Kiss make-up on, and run
right across all the lanes screaming, "Get up and get your Grandma
outta here!"

slang

choose your words more carefully.

We're flying down Forest Lane in the GTO past all these
lame people. We're going ~~fucking~~ wild and everybody is freaking
out on us. All these cars full of beautiful girls keep pulling up
next to us and we're all going, "for my money you can't be too
soon, meet you greet you in the ladies room." And "plaster caster
grab hold of me faster." They're all trying to get us to pull over
and party but we just keep rocking out.

Then this fucking 454 pick-up full about (ten) huge rednecks

Ten in one truck? Avoid exaggeration.

pulls up and they're hating us and calling us (fags) so we take off.
At about 60. *MPH.?* The duct tape on the hood busts and the cool McDonald's
hood scoop flies off and hits the red neck's truck. I pull a
quick 180 and slide out. The GTO jumps the curb and plows down
about 30 feet of somebody's nice suburban fence. I guess the red
necks figured we were in enough shit *use a better word.* and took off. A bedroom light
goes on in the house just as we're pulling out, and the GTO
leaves a pair of beautiful positraction rooster tails in the lawn.
We stupidly *Yes!* cruise back to McDonald's to play some more air
guitar and brag about the chase. Then this Richardson cop pulls
up. He checks out the front of the GTO and the hood's got all
this duct tape on it and the grille is fucking full of busted
wooden fence shit. So he walks in real show and spots us sitting
in the corner booth all fucking dressed up like the stupidest
band in the world and I'm just going, "I gotta laugh cause I
know I'm gonna die."

We definitely need a parent-teacher conference.

D-

Please have your parents sign and return this essay.

Are you trying to stay back a year?

"Its a Smoked World After All"

By Michelle Burroughs

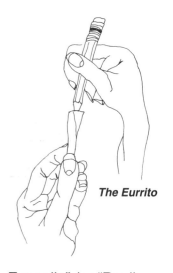

The Duece

The Eurrito

It's a great big wonderful world we live in. It's a world of laughter, a world of hope, a world of fun and a world of dope. There's so much here to share that it's time we're aware it's a smoked world after all.

Across the globe the initiated are twisting and sparking up to their heart's content. The London Underground scene has not forgotten power to the flower. In the cafes of Amsterdam they're getting snake-eyed and lazy. The chic and elite in Wiesbaden,

Germany are blowin' the froth off their lagers and turning numbers with a smile. Even way down under our brother and sisters in Australia are plumed and fumed, poised for the perfect hazey buzz. Without going into great detail, let's check into how the other half lights.

The classic European joint, "The Continental," is the hands down fave for the hipsters of London and Amsterdam. The marijuana is mixed with tobacco for better

rolling consistency and smokeability...I think. True, the stash foes further but through actual experience, it ruins the 'soul glory' that is the taste and sensation of marijuana.

The skin is folded at an angle, topped off and twisted. The wider end must be tipped vertically then capped like the silo of a missile. It's cute, has a candy cane striped effect but ultimately will just make you woozy unless you're accustomed to the deal.

The "Hail Mary," or "The

Zeppelin" (or "Really Good Year Blimp") is another international standard. Two skins are glued at an angle and the same technique, as in the preceding paragraph, is applied. Before setting and settling the "Tobbaccojuana" hodge podge, a matchbook filter is tucked into the twisted end of the Eurrito (i.e. European Burrito). Overachievers fasten an additional strip of paper tot he filtered version is sans angle, tobacco and inane cardboard matchbook filter. Twin skins are glued for straight length and packing capability; big and beautiful like this great coun-

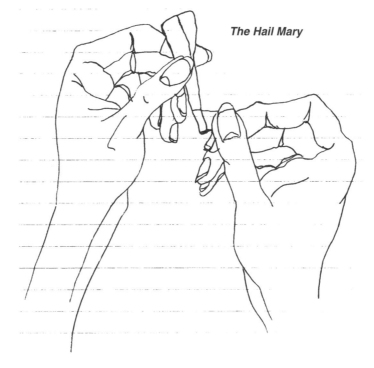

The Hail Mary

try we all call America!! One thing that is plentiful overseas that we as young Americans can be envious of is the presence and proliferation of hashish. Our industrious German and Danish brethren have developed "The Lollipoppy." A Zeppelin is rolled with an end left fairly shallow and somewhat wider a pocket of crushed hash, which is packed/wadded into a separate paper and tucked into the opening. The module is lit slowly and joyously filtered through the doob. The amounts of tobacco, marijuana and hashish depend entirely on the individual; tainting the dope is strictly in the "mind of the beroller."
 The "Deuce" is an Australian concept: two grand old American

The All-American

twist tops are lodged into a Zeppelin and secured by yet another rolling paper. The result is a wondrous peace sign looking creation, a definite 'V' for victory. The double doob seems extravagant at first, but depending on the company or partner, it proves visually appealing and a crowd pleaser. It isn't long before everybody's "oohing" and "aaahing" their way into a refined state of quiet delirium. Some interesting twists on joint rolling from our buds across the water. Amaze and entertain your friends with these new concepts. Better yet...stick with those bicentennial rolling leaves, purge your stash of sticks and stems, pack/lick/curl and get high/high/high. Bye.

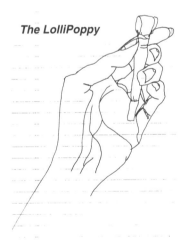

The LolliPoppy

The Rebel Yell

ROBERT E. LEE HIGH SCHOOL

THE DEVIL STILL MAKES HOLLYWOOD DO IT

November, 1975

by Cynthia Dunn

Unless you were hiding in a cave somewhere, I'm sure you knew of, and/or were in attendance at the big Halloween party that was held at the local drive-in, where THE EXORCIST, BEYOND THE DOOR, and IT'S ALIVE! played as a triple feature to thrill and chill all the "ghosts and goblins" into an "unforgettable night of terror." It was more like a completely forgettable night of laughter, or in my case, boredom, than terror. I never understood what the big deal was in the first place with THE EXORCIST when I saw it for the first time about a year ago out of curiosity after I had read the book. I remember Jodi Kerr kept telling me, "You gotta read this, you gotta read this — it's sooo scary you won't be able to sleep at night!" Then another friend said that he saw it when he went to visit his uncle, and the film was so scary, that the theater ushers were passing out "barf bags" to the audience. Well, the book wasn't really scary, and the movie was a big disappointment, as well. What's so scary about fake vomit that looks like unheated pea soup? Or a little girl who floats above her bed, cursing her lungs out like a sailor, and has a pizza face that 10 cases of pimple cream couldn't cure in a million years? Absolutely nothing, and the same goes for BEYOND THE DOOR , which is a cheap, badly dubbed rip-off of THE EXORCIST (complete with that awful, fake green pea soup vomit), and IT'S ALIVE!, which is about some "devil baby" with fangs, as it crawls and gnaws its way through a neighborhood. I suppose Hollywood thinks that we need these sort of "demon movies" for cheap thrills to entertain us in our "dull little lives," as there seems to be no end in sight of these type of movies. However, the truth of the matter is that Hollywood would rather keep raking-in the cash at the box office by churning out these products of folklore and religious superstition, and presenting them as the ultimate representations of "evil," than to have the nerve to show the true nature of evil, the face of the real devil, and what and where hell really is. Man is the real devil, and all the evils of war, annihilation, hatred and prejudice that he inflicts upon his brothers and sisters here on earth is the real hell. So, fellow students, until Hollywood can start presenting a true picture of evil in movies, I urge you — as I intend to do — to boycott these stupid "demon movies." It's high time that Hollywood stopped having its devil's food cake and eating it, too.

THE EXORCIST BARF BAG

"IF THE DEVIL MAKES YOU DO IT"

WASHINGTON

August 9, 1974

Dear Mr. Secretary:

I hereby resign the Office of President of the United States.

Sincerely,

Richard Nixon

The Honorable Henry A. Kissinger
The Secretary of State
Washington, D. C. 20520

FAILURE IS ITS

REPRINTED BY PERMISSION OF
DON CONGDON ASSOCIATES, INC.
COPYRIGHT © 1976 BY CRAIG KARPEL

"The United States are destined either to surmount the gorgeous history of feudalism, or else prove the most tremendous failure of time."
— Walt Whitman,
Democratic Vistas.

Welcome to 1976, Year of the Turkey. As fife, drum and flag combos with chili sauce on their bandages march through the shopping malls of our fair land, I am here to say a few words about how everything and everybody has bombed, flunked, stiffed, flopped and otherwise gone down the tube. I'm talking about failure, friends and neighbors. That's right, the dirtiest word beginning with F in the English language. It's amazing that they'll let me write about it in a family magazine. I mean, you could get on Johnny Carson and say, "I had leukemia," and they'd cheer. If you said, "I had V.D.," they'd all be shouting "Hi-yo!" But if you sat down, crossed your legs and said, "I am a failure" — absolute silence. Johnny would do his million-dollar deadpan take, clear his throat and tease a dog-food commercial. After the break, you'd be in the second seat, turkey.

Usually when I begin to think about whipping up a socioliterary confection, the muse is good to me and the information I need meets me halfway. If I need some material for a package on male sexuality, some stud will sidle up to me and confide that his chocolate bar has melted. If I'm looking for telephone tidbits, books fall open to ribald tales about Alexander G. Bell. But I was entirely unprepared for the pleonasm of helpful hints that the world gave me when I started thinking about failure. *Commentary* came out with a symposium on "America Now: A Failure of Nerve?" *The Village Voice* reviewed *Nashville* and *Ragtime* under the banner, "FAILURE-OF-AMERICA FAD." George C. Scott revived Arthur Miller's epic drama of failure, *Death of a Salesman. Time* started a section called "Failures." I opened *Nestor Kraly's Amazing Sports Records & Other Oddities* and read this quote: "'I always turn to the sports page first. The sports page records people's accomplishments; the front page has nothing but man's failures, - former Chief Justice Earl Warren."

So I turned to the sports page and there was a story about the record number of baseball-team managers that had been told to take a walk. I opened the *New York Daily News* and there was Linda McCartney, saying, "My dad went to Harvard, my mother went to Smith and my brother went to Stanford. They really thought I was a failure." You've never seen Linda on the Carson show, have you? I turned on the television for some karmic relief. Eric Sevareid appeared and started complaining to me about "failures and neurotics in the news." At first I thought he was talking about Henry Kissinger. Then I figured out that he was actually miffed at Sally Quinn for her book. It's all about failure — hers — with *CBS Morning News*. I escaped to a 65th-floor cocktail party at New York's Rainbow Grill, but my editor at PLAYBOY cornered me and asked how the piece was coming. "Words fail," quoth I. I could not bear to tell him the awful truth: that my journey to the center of failure was proving to be an unqualified success.

Let us now praise famous turkeys. The Best and the Brightest get the Failure of the Era Award for the Indochina war, which, fortunately, closed out of town. The US. and its allies fought

1976

AND THE
HAPPINESS

CENTRAL INTELLIGENCE AGENCY

OWN REWARD

continuously in Asia starting in 1942 to see whether or not the West would get to boss the industrialization of the East. European civilization, which had been pushing Westward for nearly half a millennium, finally got stiff-armed once and for all in 1975. Vietnam is the focal point of American failure. Everybody who's anybody has failed there. The diplomatic corps failed to avert the war in the first place. The CIA failed to figure out what was going on. The press failed to drive home the reality of the war. The hawks failed to win the war. The movement failed to end the war. Two Presidents failed to convince us we were winning. The Justice Department failed to convict Daniel Ellsberg. The right failed to pin the blame for bugging out on the left. The airlift failed. Even the anticlimax failed: The Mayaguez incident's 41 dead was a grotesque price to pay for 39 captive seamen. And just to make sure we didn't mar our Vietnam record with even one small triumph, we failed to welcome the refugees.

Fortunately, we were distracted from the enormity of our failure in Indochina by the failure of the American politi-

cal system. Watergate began with the failure of George McGovern to make the break - in a campaign issue. After all, if McGovern had won, Nixon wouldn't have had us to kick around anymore, right? Nixon's attempt at an Executive coup failed. Hunt, McCord, Mitchell, Dean, Agnew, Strachan, Magruder, Young, Colson, Kalmbach all failed. Nixon's ugly career finally failed. The President failed the Presidency. The Presidency, which he thought of as a shield, failed Nixon. The Presidency, which we had thought of as the epitome of success, failed us. Congress' attempt to impeach Nixon failed. Jaworski's attempt to bring Nixon before the bar of justice failed. And the failed President was replaced by the first man in history to succeed to the Presidency without having to succeed.

Congress has failed to override Gerald Ford's veto so many times that the nation is to all intents being ruled autocratically by a nonelected pseudo President. The CIA has failed in its primary mission: to keep its own activities under wraps. The amnesty program for antiwar heroes has failed. The dumbass WIN campaign was a

failure, but no more so than the Government's entire anti-inflation campaign, from price controls on down.

And everything else has failed. For instance, New York has failed. Environmentalists have failed to stop the Alaska Pipeline. Squeaky failed, not to mention Sara Jane. In fact, it was the first two times in history that the Secret Service *and* a would-be assassin *both* failed. Paul Schrade's campaign to reopen the Robert Kennedy assassination case failed. England has failed. Ruffian broke down in the back-stretch. The state of North Carolina failed to convict Joan Little — things are getting bad when a Southern state can't even nail a black woman who stabs a white man in the back with an ice pick while his pants are off. With Joe Colombo crippled, Joey Gallo iced, Sam Giancana wasted, Meyer Lansky and Angelo Bruno of Philly sick, Raymond Patriarca of New England on parole, Cosa Nostra is now *coso fallito*. The colleges and universities have failed. Ten years ago, they were riding high on post-Sputnik Federal largess and war-baby tuitions. Now they can't even pay their electric bills. And just when democracy is fail-

continued page 120

| END OF SCHOOL | # The Rebel Yell | FINAL ISSUE |

VOLUME 21 ISSUE 9 **ROBERT E. LEE HIGH SCHOOL** **MAY 16, 1976**

What the Bicentennial Means to Us

— by Tony Olson and Mike Newhouse

SPECIAL FOR THE REBEL YELL NEWS

Like a cowboy shooting a man in the back, a young United States gained it's independence using guerrilla warfare, ambushing English troops who were used to marching and fighting in a conservative "pause, fire, reload, march" formation. Easy pickings for a country desperate to maintain its freedom and independence.

Since the original American Revolution in 1776, it seems the US has continued it's long history of using sly, and often underhanded methods to maintain it's independence. With the questionable ethics of the CIA, and the dorks of Watergate, President Ford set up the Rockefeller Commission, a panel investigating possible illegal domestic operations of the CIA (domestic operations are left to the FBI, the CIA deals mainly with foreign operations).

With the findings of the Rockefeller Commission investigating CIA activities, there seems to be a close relationship between the CIA and the Mafia.

Now that the CIA is under the close scrutiny of the public eye, and it can be regarded as an organization of pirates using pirates to achieve it's goals. Using the Mafia and organized crime "because of their expertise and contacts that were not available to law-abiding citizens," the CIA covers all the ground it needs to cover-up.

During the investigation, Ford expanded the role of the Rockefeller Commission to include an inquiry into the CIA's alleged plots to kill foreign leaders.

In Las Vegas during the mid-sixties a break-in was reported in the suite of Dan Rowen (later co-star of Rowen and Martin's Laugh-In). The criminal was apprehended and claimed he was a private investigator, working for a Florida detective agency, investigating Phyllis McGuire's relationship with Mr. Rowen. When confronted with who hired him, the Florida agency told the authorities to contact the CIA.

Here, it was discovered, that Phyllis McGuire was the girlfriend of gangster Sam Giancana. As a favor to Giancana, the CIA helped keep tabs on his girlfriend, one of the singing McGuire sisters, whom he suspected was seeing comedian Dan Rowen. Later, in the investigation, there were unconfirmed reports that a wire-tap in her room was O.K.'d by then Attorney General Robert Kennedy.

But we wondered why would the CIA waste their time spying on the girlfriends of Mafia leaders. Then the truth came out, or should we say "leaked out," in the shape of a conspiracy to assassinate Fidel Castro in the early 1960s.

Under President Kennedy, officials in the White House examined the question of assassinating Castro, as a possible solution to the "Cuban problem" in 1961 and 1962. White House officials talked of "how nice it would be if this or that" leader wasn't around anymore. These White House thoughts resulted in "contingency planning at CIA." (Contingency means "an event conceived of as a possible occurrence in the future," in other words, manipulation of future events).

continued page 118

STARSKY

& HUTCH

NAME: David Soul
BIRTH DATE: Aug. 28, 1943
BIRTH PLACE: Chicago, Illinois
HAIR: Blond
EYES: Blue
SIGN: Virgo
TV CHARACTER: Detective Ken "Hutch" Hutchinson in *Starsky and Hutch*
PAST CHARACTERS: Joshua Bolt on *Here Come the Brides*; as Makara in the *Star Trek* episode "The Apple"; Ted Warrick on *Owen Marshall, Counselor at Law*; insane cop in Clint Eastwood film *Magnum Force*.
FEELINGS ABOUT SERIES: "It's wonderful."
VICES: Chain smoking cigarettes, drinking lots of coffee, arguing religious theology with friends (his father was a Lutheran minister).
HOBBIES: Playing guitar, writing songs
PRESENT PLAYTHING: Lynne Marta, who he met on set of *Owen Marshall*

NAME: Paul Michael Glaser
BIRTH DATE: March 25, 1943
BIRTH PLACE: Cambridge, Massachusetts
HAIR: Brown
EYES: Blue
SIGN: Aries
TV CHARACTER: Detective Dave Starsky on *Starsky and Hutch*
WHAT HE COULD HAVE BEEN: An architect like his dad
COLLEGE DAYS: Got a Master's degree in Theater and English from Tulane University and a Master of Arts degree in acting and directing from Boston University.
HOW HE GOT INTO SHOWBIZ: After playing in summer stock and off-Broadway in New York, he landed a role on the soap opera *Love of Life*, which led to other TV roles.
FILM CREDITS: Perchik in *Fiddler on the Roof* and Ralph in *Butterflies Are Free*
FEELINGS ABOUT SERIES: "The scripts are retarded."
PAST HOBBIES: Used to be so uptight he'd punch holes in walls.
HOBBIES: Tennis, guitar playing, motorcycles, yoga, his dog Max
FAVORITE MOTORCYCLE: The same one he had before he was a star—still rides it.

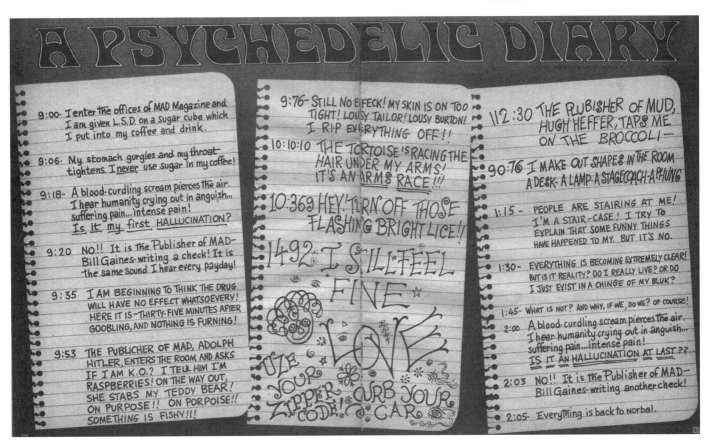

boy

friends

Jodi Kramer

Early musical fave: TV's *Banana Splits*, particularly Fleagle, the floppy dog who drives a little dune buggy as well as sings pop tunes.

Early idols: Bobby Sherman, David Cassidy.

Remote mentor: Judy Bloom, author of <u>Are You There, God, It's Me, Margaret</u>, a frank, open discussion of all the stuff their mothers neglected to tell their daughters freely and openly.

Eye-opener: Warren Beatty's *Shampoo*, a movie she thinks is kind of creepy and boring until near the end, when George the oversexed hairdresser talks about how men spend so much time trying to nail women, how women love them for it and hate them for it, and how he can't help himself because women are so, well, great. The speech clarifies a lot of feelings Jodi hasn't been able to express.

Accomplishments: Executes a perfect herkey (leap into air with one leg bent) on her first attempt at summer cheerleading camp. Authors a cheer frequently used to support the Robert E. Lee Rebels, "Spirit, drive, ability— we're the best as you can see! So shout it out with all yer might, fight fight fight!"

Regrets: Not going steady with Randy Floyd; not having a little sister she could help through the incredible bullshit teenage girls have to endure.

Favorite stuffed collectible: A troll doll Pink stole at the senior fair. He had already spent $2.17 in pocket change trying to get the lima bean in the frog's mouth.

Favorite cruising cocktail: A Dairy Queen "Mr. Misty" and Bacardi 151 that goes down like milk.

Theme song: Bee Gees "Nights On Broadway" and KC and the Sunshine Band's "That's The Way (I Like It)."

Shoe News Now

by Jodi Kramer

Steppin' Out

1. All tied up in sexy sandals

2. Wedgie platforms and straw covered heels.

3. Mom's dress shoes— don't borrow!

4. Womper Stompers, Earth Shoes, and Dexters are all popular choices for shoes with thick rubber soles.

5. Huarachi sandals with wooden heels squeak when you walk.

6. Platform shoe with 5 inch heel, illegal to drive with these in Oklahoma.

7. The Gangster! Steppin' out on the disco floor.

8. Head for the new disco in these men's platforms.

9. Buffalo sandals are great with toe socks in the winter.

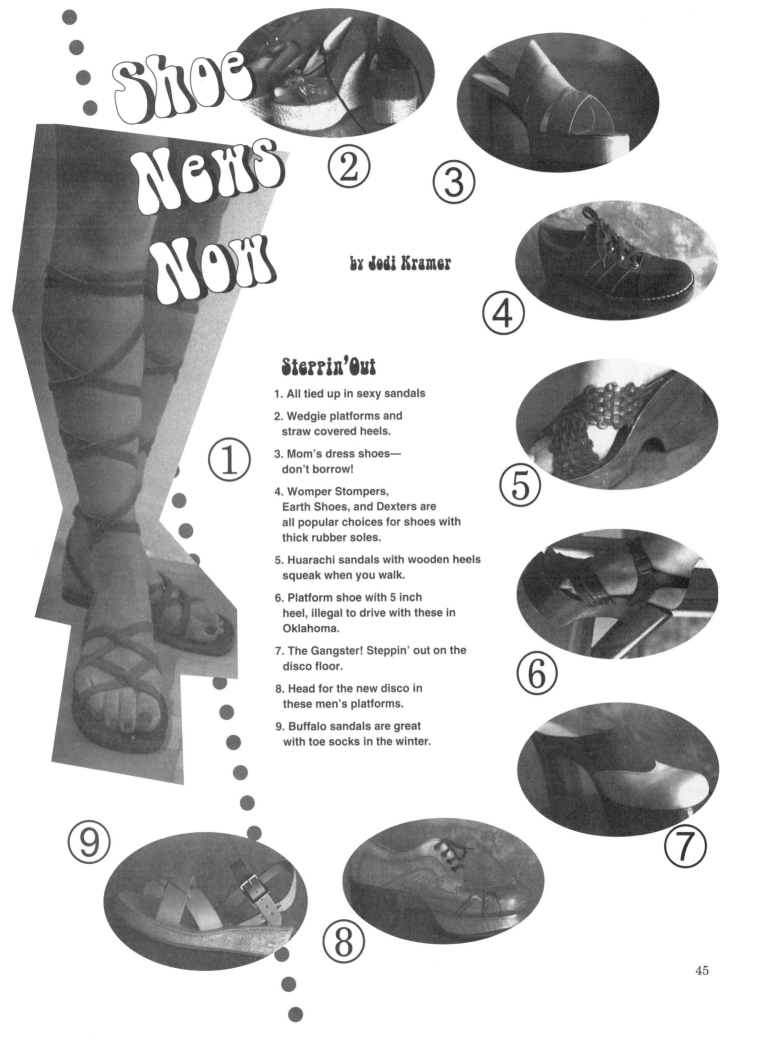

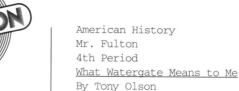

Tony Olson

Prized possession: A photo of Tony shaking hands with George McGovern.

Sacred tomes: Norman Mailer's chronicles of sixties politics, <u>Armies of the Night</u> and <u>Miami and the Siege of Chicago</u>.

Just a coincidence? On November 22, 1973 ten years to the hour of the Kennedy assassination, Tony is in a theater watching *Executive Action*, the ultimate J.F.K. conspiracy movie.

Adventure in the Fourth Estate: Fired up by Woodward and Bernstein's <u>All the President's Men</u>, Tony collaborates with Mike Newhouse on an intensive investigation of the secret activities of the C.I.A. for the *Rebel Yell*.

Delicious Dilemma: Can't decide if Kristy McNichol would make a better girlfriend, sister, or study buddy.

Wall Posters: "Hang in there baby" and a life size door hanging of Jon Voight in "Midnight Cowboy."

Favorite character on the Mary Tyler Moore Show: Rhoda. She's quick with a wry comeback, deeply cares for her mother's well-being and supports herself in the cut-throat hyper competitive world of window dressing.

Secret Fashion Risk: To wear a bicentennial scarf tied in a nice ascot in the Oscar Wilde vain. Taking it off only while roaming the halls between classes and during gym of course.

Favorite rock critics: Greil Marcus, the sage of Berkeley, and Lester Bangs, the mad stomper from Detroit. Since Tony is the only kid at school who bases his buying decisions on reviews, he is also the first one to get Bruce Springsteen's *Born to Run*, Neil Young's *Zuma*, and Dylan's *Blood on the Tracks*. Also loves Randy Newman, and gets voluminous hate mail for his review in the Rebel Yell calling Led Zep's *Physical Graffiti* "a pretentious mass of overproduced bong water."

American History
Mr. Fulton
4th Period
<u>What Watergate Means to Me</u>
By Tony Olson

"Our long national nightmare is over," said Gerald Ford when he assumed the presidency from Richard Nixon. All the reporters and television commentators seemed to agree with him, judging by the number of times they repeated the words "national nightmare." Me, I'm not convinced. Maybe Ford should have said, "Our national horror picture show is over." And maybe David Brinkley should have cocked his head and quipped, "President Ford may have meant the Watergate scandal, but one could be pardoned for thinking he was referring to the entire Nixon presidency," (the line delivered with Brinkley's familiar cracker barrel rhythm).

If Nixon can be pardoned for wiping himself with the constitution, then please pardon me for thinking Watergate was great entertainment. I was vacationing with my family in the Pacific Northwest when the Ervin Committee came on the tube, and neither miles of ocean nor bra-less college girls could tear me away from the hearings on TV for very long. Nixon's henchmen seemed to combine the character traits of all the shifty salesmen and eerie executives I've ever met at wedding receptions and cocktail parties: on top of the world one day, squirming in the hot seat the next. It left Hollywood in the dust, that's for sure. Sam Ervin was Jimmy Stewart grown bulbous with indignation. John Dean was Don Knotts turned zombie stool pigeon. God, it was fun.

Does this sound cynical? Well, look at it from a generational perspective. My parents and their generation grew up with Franklin Roosevelt, Harry S. Truman, Dwight Eisenhower and John Kennedy: presidents who provided bold leadership (except for Eisenhower, who apparently spent most of his time golfing and reading Westerns) and didn't routinely lie to the public. My generation grew up with Lyndon Johnson, a strange, long-suffering man who walked into the Vietnam disaster like he was starring in a Texas version of Hamlet, and Richard Nixon, a seriously weird human being.

After spending my childhood in the sixties — a carnival ride between assassinations and featuring acid, orgies and loud guitars — maybe you'll forgive me for expecting bizarre drama every time I turn on the news. As Watergate turned into an incredible maze of corruption and crime, my parents were shocked. I was just fascinated. Nixon had secretly bombed, then invaded, Cambodia, a neutral country. He won the election after his Good German told everybody peace was at hand, then celebrated Christmas by bombing Hanoi. For him, obstructing justice and talking into Oval Office tape recorders about "cold-cocking the bastards" was all in a day's work. Presidents, after

continued page 118

WATERGATE TRIVIA QUIZ

Reprinted from *National Lampoon* "Watergate Trivia" by Christopher Cerf and Bill Effros

Match the description with the appropriate name...

The answers are at the bottom of the page. You're on the honor system, and there's no time like the present to apply the lessons of Watergate — cheat!

1. He testified: "I will let the answer stand- whatever it was."

2. His only known hobby is taking and showing home movies of Richard Nixon.

3. He allegedly manhandled Martha Mitchell and held her downwhile a doctor gave her an injection to keep her from talking.

4. Before gaining an important position in the Nixon administration, he owned gambling casinos in Las Vegas.

5. Whom did the president call a "candy-ass?"

6. Who, to quote Richard Nixon, is an "asshole," "a little nuts," and "just isn't well-screwed on?"

7. He put forth the "sinister force" theory to explain the eighteen-and-a-half minute gap on the tape.

Match Up
H. R. Haldeman
George Shultz
Gordon Liddy
Fred Larue
Richard Moore
Steve King
Alexander Haig

continued page 119

Answers:
Match Up
1. Richard Moore
2. H. R. Haldeman
3. Steve King
4. Fred Larue
5. George Shultz
6. Gordon Liddy
7. Alexander Haig

True or False
1. True
2. True
3. True
4. True
5. True
6. True
7. True
8. True
9. True
10. True

Helpful Hints

"I Don't Know What You're Talkin' About, Dad"
(Or Smoking Pot At Home)

by Kevin Pickford

Recently it's been brought to my attention that a lot of my friends have been getting busted for smoking pot, in the privacy of their own homes! Now, I don't mean by the fuzz, or anything like that. You see, at least the cops have to have a search warrant to go through your room and your personal belongings. No, there's a much more bogus menace out there, and it usually answers to the call of "dad!!!"

You see, there is a special power that your mom and dad have because they can enter your room any time they want, (usually when you're at school) and do an illegal search on your whole room. And I mean everywhere, from the back of your closet, through your desk, to under your mattress. What can you do about it? Absolutely nothing. The mere mention of you asking if they searched your room will immediately arouse suspicion, as though you have something to hide in the first place. So much for personal privacy; they think it is their right to look at everything you've written while they search for Satan.

Ever since I got that first lecture from mom about me smelling like pot (I told her it was my friends incense), I decided to take some precautions to insure the safety of my allowance, because that's how I'm buying my weed in the first place.

The first thing I had to do was cut down on all the cool paraphernalia I was getting, and man, like that was a big drag. It was starting to get hard trying to hide my three-foot bong, my Power Hitter™ chamber pipe with adjustable chambers, smokeless pipes, a U.S. Bong™, smoke stones, a bullet-shaped roach clip, rolling machines, pocket scales, and my NORML membership.

The next step was finding a good hiding place. Then it hit me: I put all the stuff out in the open continued page 119

KEVIN PICKFORD

Born: To Chuck Pickford, former Army drill instructor and current president of First National Bank, the same bank where Kevin, Don, and "Pink" steal two Spirit of '76 bicentennial statues and paint them to look like Kiss's Gene Simmons and Peter Criss. Mom is Eileen Pickford, who has a blind spot where Kevin is concerned. If not for her, he would've been sent to military school long ago.

Musical Karma: Kevin dedicates himself to getting high, throwing parties and collecting unlistenable "progressive" and acid rock albums. He fills his record shelves with the works of Uriah Heep, King Crimson, McDonald & Giles, Emerson, Lake & Palmer, Robin Trower, Hawkwind, Magma, Gentle Giant, Triumvirate, Genesis and Yes. He compares Tales of Topographic Oceans to Bach and Beethoven in a paper for Music Appreciation and receives a D+.

Stereo System: Dual turntable, Pioneer 50-watt receiver, JBL speakers. Saving up for a pair of massive Klipschorns. Contemplates switching over from 8-tracks to cassettes.

Close Call: After hosting a two-kilo party while his parents are in Florida, he cleans up so well they can't find evidence to go with the pungent odor clinging to the drapes.

Wall Posters: M.C. Escher's drawing of nightingales turning into table napkins, Salvador Dali's painting of liquid bank vaults, and a pre-psychedelic mural by Heronymous Bosch.

Vocation: Inherits the Robert E. Lee dope dealing franchise from a senior who's arrested in Operation Intercept, Nixon's drug interdiction program.

Favorite Pastime: Trying to be the coolest guy in the crowd.

Prized Possession: The Judge, a 1970 GTO he gets for his 16th birthday.

Quote of the Year: "Keep on space truckin."

Turning Pot Into Hash

With the price of good weed sky-rocketing to almost thirty bills a lid, it's time to step back, light up a boagie, and assess the situation at hand. Many solutions can easily be applied to this inflationary problem; quit smoking pot, for example, or rip off your pot dealer.

But being a high connoisseur, not to mention having a life-time subscription to *High Times*, I saved up all my money and invested in a real cool Isomerizer™ and joined the spaced age.

As an investment, I've already made back more then double the money I spent on it in the first place by selling "Mexican hash" or should I say "Ixxachiachan Blonde." I even sent a picture to *High Times* of my hash fingers lying next to some castanets and a wrestling mask (but they didn't use it, so I figure that everybody's doing the same with their ISO, and maybe some day I'll get the center page...).

So anyway, below are some guidelines about how to use an ISO, mainly because you guys are always borrowing it and I'm tired of explaining how to use it every time. All you need is a bag of lousy shake to get you started, and I'll be more than happy to sell you some.

Isomerization

1. Take your pot and grind it into as fine a powder as possible. Dry it in the oven some, if necessary to improve your grinding consistency. Take processed pot and put in a regular sized coffee filter and place it in the center holder of isomerizer.

2. Measure out two pints of denatured alcohol, then soak the pot grounds and pour the rest into bottom of isomerizer. Put the top on and fill the trough with water. Turn on ISO about 3/4's of the way.

When the ISO light is on this means the bottom's heating. The alcohol vaporizes and rises. The top of the ISO is a condenser so it's important to keep the trough full of water, otherwise the alcohol will evaporate.

3. Leave ISO on high like this for about ten to twelve hours. The alcohol is condensing and dripping through the grounds. As it passes through the pot it's extracting the oils and leaving the oil in the bottom as it vaporizes and condenses all over again. After the first six hours or so you may want to stir the grinds around some to insure maximum extraction. Attention!! Before you open the ISO for any reason, turn it off for about ten minutes and let it cool some. You're dealing with hot 100% alcohol fumes. No smoking or other flames or sparks while ISO top is off. After the first ten to twelve hours turn the heat down to about four and let it go for another twenty-four hours. Now take pot out and gently squeeze out as much alcohol out of pot as possible and pour back into ISO.

At this point, what you have is all the oil that was originally in the pot mixed with the alcohol in the bottom of the ISO. The oil is where all the THC and chlorophyll along with any other

extractables are. This means that at this point the pot grinds are essentially useless unless you want to use them for a variation that will be discussed later, besides re-selling it...

If you look in the bottom, what you should see is a marbleized liquor with a deep rich color the hue of the particular pot you're using. Man!! Is it pretty! But don't drink it!!

4. Place a Pyrex container where the filter was. This is to reclaim the alcohol. It is very important to measure the alcohol before you put it in so you can reclaim the same amount. And you'll end up reclaiming almost exactly the same amount you put in before except for the little bit in the grinds and the small amount that vaporizes while the top's off.

At this point, it's time to really pay attention. You can crank the heat as fast as you want as you want to reclaim. But when you get down to that last 1/2 cup you'd better slow her way down, and keep a careful eye. This is the point where you want to make sure you got all the alcohol, but you don't want to burn the pot!! Unless it's in a glass pipe, you're ready to kick back. If you notice white

continued page 124

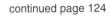

HighWitnessNews

WEED RUNS WILD

Thousands of acres of wild pot are spreading over West Virginia and authorities there are busy trying to control it. During W.W.'s I and II the West Virginia eastern panhandle provided hemp for rope factories, but the current crop is up for grabs.

In 1972, the West Virginia Department of Agriculture was given the job of destroying the rapidly growing wild weed. An initial aerial survey showed 2,000 acres of marijuana growing wild and Agriculture Commissioner Gus Douglas estimated it would take five years to destroy them all. However, while project leader Robert Frame reports the work is running according to schedule, his figures indicate that

The High And Mighty

In the wake of the David Carradine pot bust there has been a wave of arrests of the great, the near great, and the once great. Rubbing elbows with the common felons and wrongdoers are the following:

•Aging 1930's movie star Lash Larue was charged with possession of marijuana after being arrested in Clayton County, Ga., for drunkenness. The former cowboy matinee idol, remembered as a whip-cracking swaggerer on screen, had a whip in his car at the time of the arrest.

•Danny Partridge was sleeping in the back seat of his car when San Francisco police arrested him and three companions for possession of marijuana. The fifteen-year-old actor in the popular series The Partridge Family was released in his parents' custody.

•Congressional Medal of Honor winner and Vietnam hero Richard Pentry has been convicted of selling cocaine in Santa Rose, Calif. Pentry — whose sentencing had to be postponed because it was first scheduled for Veterans Day — saved scores of wounded GIs from a Viet Cong attack.

•One of the best-known jockeys in racing, Larry Adams, was arrested for possession of marijuana and codeine sulphate pills at Newark International Airport.

•New Jersey Representative Charles W. Sandman's nineteen-year-old son Robert S. Sandman was indicted by a grand jury in Atlantic County for possession of more than two pounds of marijuana with intent to distribute.

•Drug Enforcement Administration agent Jon Alan Ercolo was arrested in Denver, Colo., on charges of selling grass he had been storing as evidence.

•In what some observers feel is an attempt to smear Sheriff Richard Hongisto of San Francisco County, a reformer who is up for re-election in 1975, inspector Cecil Pharris arrested Deputy Sheriff Larry Burris on charges of selling cocaine to prisoners at San Francisco County Prison. No drugs or paraphernalia were found in Burris's possession and he was released on his own recognizance.

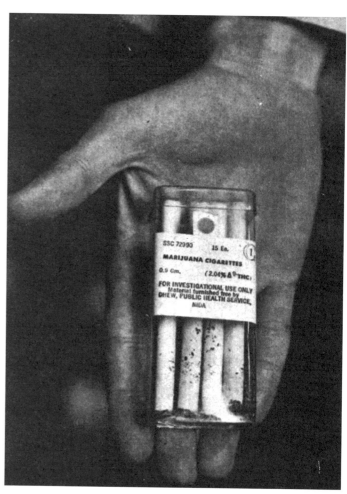

Courtesy *High Times*

HighWitnessNews

so far in 1974 his crews have worked 111 separate marijuana tracts comprising 3,981 acres.

"Marijuana was even growing on the golf course at Moorefield," Douglas said.

CARTER KID FAVORS FARM POT

First son Jeff Carter, 27, an admitted doper, believes that American farmers should take the lead in cannabis agriculture. The move would prevent the public from spending millions on foreign imports, Carter told Gatewood Galbraith on a campaign swing through Kentucky last October.

Galbraith, 29, is president and founder of the Future Kentucky Marijuana Growers Association (FKMGA), a group devoted to organizing and promoting full-scale cannabiculture throughout the United States.

During their brief meeting, the pair discussed the legalization of the cash crop, citing tax revenues as a major justification. Reported Galbraith, "Carter agreed with our position on domestic cultivation and said legalization was "necessary" Galbraith intends to "go right to the White House" with a proposal for a domestic pot-farming lobby.

Killer Weed Thrives in Classroom

Marijuana has been discovered growing in the fourth-grade classrooms in Riverton, Wyoming.

Thirty-two youngsters and at least two teachers and administrators were exposed to the dangerous pot, but no casualties were cited. Riverton Police investigationg the incident said that no one knew what the plant was for at least four or five months. Seeds dropped into the soil in September were reputedly geraniums-a class project that died-while the reefer bloomed and even flowered.

U.S.-APPROVED POT

Bob Randall, the only person in the US. with government permission to get high on pot, holds a 15-joint pack of Uncle Sam's personal stash, grown at the government pot farm in Mississippi and containing 2.04 percent THC. Randall smokes a pack a week since a judge ruled that he needs the weed in the treatment of his glaucoma.

POTAGANDA

Tapes yielded by former President Nixon to the House Judiciary Committee reveal that television, movies and radio were targeted for an onslaught of anti-drug messages. In one taped conversation between Nixon and domestic advisor John D. Ehrlichmann, they discuss the now defunct CBS series "O'Hara—The US. Treasury" starring David Janssen. Ehrlichman told Nixon, "You know, we got, us, a narcotics show on.... it had a hell of a rating its first, uh, time." Nixon called the program "a good show." He seemed impressed with its style. "My God, they had, uh, they had guys chasing people with, uh, airplanes and all that sort of thing" he said.

Jim Moser, a writer for "O'Hara," recalled that at a 1970 White House Conference on Drug Abuse, 35 media executives from the television networks

The police deparment will not press charges, but it has started work on a drug awareness program so that officials in the school system will be able to recognize the plant.

and California production studios were encouraged to play up the drug problem and get the government message across. Moser recalled, "It was remarkable. They took writers and producers back to Washington to see how we could push the anti-drug thing. John Mitchell told me 'Get in and write some fine scripts, boy'!"

The producer of "O'Hara," Leonard Kaufman admitted to being aware of secret agreements between government and Hollywood. He says "it was a political thing for productions to expose the drug problem."

"O'Hara" folded after one dismal season before the American public.

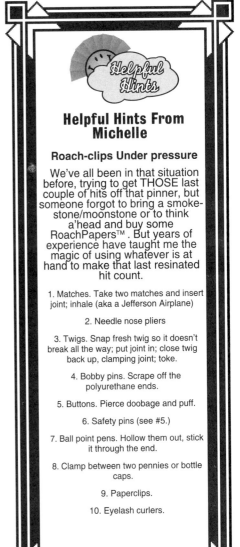

Helpful Hints From Michelle

Roach-clips Under pressure

We've all been in that situation before, trying to get THOSE last couple of hits off that pinner, but someone forgot to bring a smoke-stone/moonstone or to think a'head and buy some RoachPapers™. But years of experience have taught me the magic of using whatever is at hand to make that last resinated hit count.

1. Matches. Take two matches and insert joint; inhale (aka a Jefferson Airplane)

2. Needle nose pliers

3. Twigs. Snap fresh twig so it doesn't break all the way; put joint in; close twig back up, clamping joint; toke.

4. Bobby pins. Scrape off the polyurethane ends.

5. Buttons. Pierce doobage and puff.

6. Safety pins (see #5.)

7. Ball point pens. Hollow them out, stick it through the end.

8. Clamp between two pennies or bottle caps.

9. Paperclips.

10. Eyelash curlers.

Pickford "The Judge"

MAKE: 1970 Pontiac GTO

DRIVEN BY: Pickford

ACQUIRED BY: Daddy's store-bought muscle car, turned hand-me-down in Sophomore year, 1974

ENGINE: L67 455 Ram Air IV with four-bolt mains

COMPRESSION RATIO: 10.5:1

HORSEPOWER: 370

8-TRACK: Pioneer ST 709 20w output

TAPES: ZZ Top "Fandango", Led Zeppelin, Pink Floyd, Black Sabbath

TRANSMISSION: Turbo 400 hydromatic

WHEELS: Factory Rally IIS

LAST TICKET RECEIVED: Doing 40 in a 20 (mph) school zone

GLOVE-BOX CONTENTS: Discarded tickets, Michelle's super gloss lipstick, photo of his brother in "Nam" currently on MIA. list, roaches, roach clips, cigarette roller, concert ticket stubs

BUMPER STICKER: "No Fat Chicks"

UNDER SEAT: Frisbee, "High Times" magazine, air freshener, Sonic ketchup packages

HANGING FROM REAR VIEW MIRROR: Feather roach clip

The Downing Of The SS. Minnow

by Shavonne Wright

Here's our blackboard summary of some of the Gilligan's Island episodes we watched this year... journalism is a great class to take. We found that all of us related to at least one of the characters on the island. For example I always felt that I was Ginger. We also discovered in our discussion that each character represented one of the Seven Deadly Sins (Jodi still says that Gilligan is one of the Seven Wonders).

The Seven Stranded Castaways

Gilligan: Sloth

Skipper: Anger

Mr. Howell: Gluttony

Mrs. Howell: Vanity

Mary Ann: Envy

Ginger: Lust

The Professor: Pride

A Selected "Gilligan's Island" Episode List

1. Gilligan Transistor Radio Mouth
2. Lagoon Mine Story
3. Invisible Lightning Rod
4. Red Menace Gilligan
5. Radioactive Harvest
6. Gill-cula
7. Unholy Matrimony
8. Bank robbers
9. Minnow Glue Boat
10. Astro Castaway
11. Witch Doctor Voodoo Dolls
12. Hurricane Hut
13. President Gilligan
14. Ginger Broadway Island
15. Exploding Nails
16. Gilligan Bug Death
17. Castaway Films
18. Penniless Howell's
19. Rock Mosquitoes Opening Band
20. Aliens on the Moon
21. Long Distance Wrong Number
22. Mind Reading Berries
23. Hawaiian Robot Walk
24. Gorilla Warfare
25. Mary Ann Boyfriend Eloper Fatality
26. Gilligan and the Beanstalk
27. Gilligan's Hungry Pet Lion
28. Two Mr. Howells
29. Gilligan Totem Pole Head

continued page 121

Robert E. Lee's board of education.

The coaching staff of Lee High School contemplate the day's events and the joys of elastic waistbands.

Simmone experiments with a new recipe; add freshmen, a smattering of ketchup, a suggestion of raw eggs and top it off with a generous heeping of flour. Stir until humiliated. Voila!!

"I.D.?? I left it in my other wallet...really. Actually I work for the city. What do I do? Uh....Mayor?

Mr. Pickford: "So you're having a party and you didn't invite your parents??"

"Clint Bruno wins the beer kissing All City Finals! Rock on Clint! Good luck at State."

Simone and Darla in yet another lipstick dilemma. Simone: "Why don't they have cigarette flavored lipstick?" Darla: "Really, that's what ends up happening anyway."

Shavonne demonstrates the versatility of her favorite roach clip.

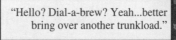

"Hello? Dial-a-brew? Yeah...better bring over another trunkload."

"Wow, so that's why they call it 'high' school. Cool!"

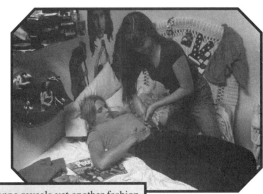

Shavonne reveals yet another fashion secret. Select your pliers carefully...

O'Bannion after tragic Clearasil explosion. The incident left 70% of his body unscarred and blemish free.

Don and Woody in heated math debate. Woody: "Of course there's six to a pack, that's why it's called a 'six-pack.'"

Ass, gas, or grass, nobody rides for free.

Paul Stanley, Bette Midler and John Denver make a guest apperance at the beer bust.

Michelle's first freehand doobie. Typing classes seem to be helpful in strengthening those nimble digits. Remember the home row!!

'676

Lee's Angels: "FREEZE TURKEY!"

Good game...good game...good game... drag you lost...good game.

PROFILES in CONFUSION

don

dawson

EARLY FOOTBALL TRAINING: Don's older brother, Dave, uses him for blocking and tackling practice as they try to recreate plays they've seen on TV. Don acquires fantastic speed and agility as he tries to avoid getting crunched.

ALTER EGO: Dresses as his idol Joe Namath for Halloween 1973, complete with fake Fu Manchu mustache.

ROLE MODEL: Burt Reynolds in The Longest Yard.

FAVORITE SCENE IN THE LONGEST YARD: Burt pops in the Skynyrd and takes off for the wet country in his recently humiliated girlfriend's car. The ride ends up in the drink and so does a bombed Burt.

SOFA SOUNDS: He devotes considerable time to finding and testing great make-out music, settling on Curtis Mayfield, The Spinner's Greatest Hits, and Jefferson Starship's "Miracles" (he can't understand how a line like "I got a taste of the real world / When I went down on you" ever got on the radio).

FANTASY SUBSTITUTE TEACHER: Star of Summer of 42' Jennifer O'Neal. During explanation of mitosis she breaks down into quiet sobbing behind her desk. After class Don offers hug and they reevaluate the "student-teacher" relationship.

POCKET CONTENTS: On key chain: bottle opener, roach clip key and gimp lace rat tail. In Navajo leather craft wallet: photo of Shavonne, ticket from ZZ Top concert, movie stub from Towering Inferno, roach wrapped in tin foil, phone number list and seven dollars and nine cents.

FASHION TRENDSETTER: First to wear bicentennial sweatband at school. First to stop wearing bicentennial sweatband realizing how dorky they looked on everybody else.

NOTABLE QUOTABLES: "It makes a Big difference if your parents are home." "I want to remember you with clothing on or not at all." "Of course I missed you baby... you weren't here."

RECENT ACCOMPLISHMENT: Never missed a concert, a workout, or game, and maintained a B-average.

THE LIGHTER SIDE OF GROOMING...

A Stolen Page from Ms. Stroud's Diaries

April 20   Explained to the kids today that we live in a <u>slave</u> society. Men take it as their right to have women serve them, defer to them, remain dependent on them, orbit them. Women demand the right to be included back into the human race! I explained that it's very important this generation fight oppressive roles — self-assertion is a political act !!!

April 23   That <u>HOT LITTLE NUMBER</u> Don Dawson tried to flirt with me again today. I swear, the second he turns 18 I'm gonna **NAIL HIM**! That'll make a <u>man</u> outta him !!!

April 30   Ran into a guy I met 10 years ago at a Love-in. As I remember, we dropped Acid and discussed universal love, and he talked about transcending this corrupt society and living in the mountains. It was great to see him again. He works for IBM now.

May 2   The big ERA rally is in Springfield Illinois this month and <u>I've got to be there</u>, but these lousy administrative drones will never stand for it. The principal still calls me "Miss" Stroud! When I explained that I ceased being "Miss" around age 16 and would prefer to be recognized as an individual, rather than identified by my relationship with a man, he said "Whoa Little Filly." I nearly **CASTRATED** him right then and there !!!

May 8   Told the kids that it doesn't matter who gets the democratic nomination, because after a <u>Crook</u> and a <u>Klutz</u>, the country is demanding a change. The democrat is going to win — simple as that. I can't believe that the conservative party would seriously consider that 2ND Rate CLOWN Ronald Reagan. Would have to be <u>brain-dead</u> to elect the guy!

May 15   MORE bicentennial flag-waving bullshit at the pep rally today. (Society insists on indoctrinating the young with this nationalistic dogma.) 200 Years of aggression and greed! And then that FROTHING NEANDERTHAL Coach Conrad brought next year's football recruits out for a bunch of inane grunting while the cheerleaders flitted around in their little skirts. I swear, giving those boys over to Coach Conrad is like putting 'em in bootcamp to be disgusting PIGS!

May 20   Called in sick and drove up to the ERA rally. Man, is was so cool to be with my sisters and demanding that discrimination <u>end</u> in our lifetime! WE WERE AN UNDENIABLE FORCE! When Illinois ratifies the bill, Indiana and Missouri will surely follow suit.... Also, did a little shopping in Springfield — bought some really BOSS suede boots! Then hit the road so I'd make it in time for school Monday.

Simone Kerr

Heroine: Cher, for having the nerve to divorce Gregg Allman after only nine days of marriage. Also admires Jackie Onassis because she doesn't let fame and money make her unhappy.

Anthem: Aerosmith's "Sweet Emotion," though in her darker moments she prefers Carly Simon's "You're So Vain."

Wheels: The 1975 AMC Pacer her parents gave her as a sixteenth birthday present, a dorky car partially redeemed by its wide body, which allows extra room to stretch in the back.

Energy source: Gallons of Dr. Pepper, supplemented by Vivarin™ dissolved in coffee especially during times of frantic activity.

Kissing aid: Peppermint or Cherry Chocolate Lip-Smacker by Bonne Bell, for "a kiss of color and a dazzling super-shine."

Favorite charm on bracelet: Sharkstooth given to her by Pink. Doesn't wear this particular jewelry around Jodi or Darla — it's mostly for around the house...

Make-up: Glossy Gel Mascara and Creamy Eye Polish by Love Cosmetics. "They glide on so perfectly you can't look overdone."

Love dilemma: Her part time squeeze, Randall "Pink" Floyd, always seems to want something more but can't ever say what it is. She gives him copies of Jonathan Livingston Seagull and The Prophet, but they don't seem to help.

Dream date: Greg Brady during his good perm period. Something silly and stupid. They'd share a buttered tub during "Jaws," catch a few dogs back at the Sonic, drive around in a station wagon listening to "The Partridge Family" (just to miff him a little bit,) and end up back at his redone sweet attic apartment room.

Dream concert: Jim Dandy of "Black Oak Arkansas" playing a solo acoustic performance. Just the man, his guitar and his music. And a cool leather vest.

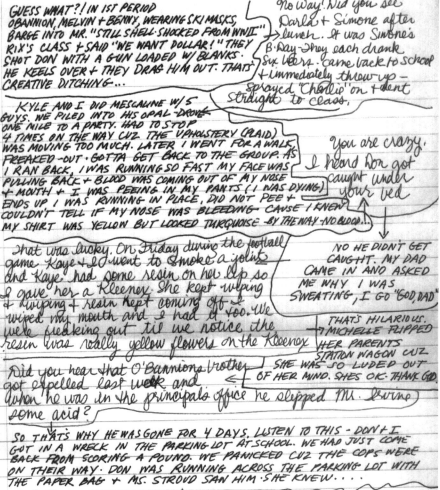

GUESS WHAT?! IN 1ST PERIOD OBANNION, MELVIN + BENNY, WEARING SKI MASKS, BARGE INTO MR. "STILL SHELL·SHOCKED FROM WWII" RIX'S CLASS + SAID "WE WANT DOLLAR!" THEY SHOT DON WITH A GUN LOADED W/ BLANKS. HE KEELS OVER + THEY DRAG HIM OUT. THAT'S CREATIVE DITCHING...

KYLE AND I DID MESCALINE W/5 GUYS. WE PILED INTO HIS OPAL·DROVE ONE MILE TO A PARTY. HAD TO STOP 4 TIMES ON THE WAY CUZ THE UPHOLSTERY (PLAID) WAS MOVING TOO MUCH. LATER I WENT FOR A WALK. FREAKED·OUT·GOTTA GET BACK TO THE GROUP. AS I RAN BACK, I WAS RUNNING SO FAST MY FACE WAS PULLING BACK + BLOOD WAS COMING OUT OF MY NOSE + MOUTH + I WAS PEEING IN MY PANTS (I WAS DYING) ENDS UP I WAS RUNNING IN PLACE, DID NOT PEE + COULDN'T TELL IF MY NOSE WAS BLEEDING- CAUSE I KNEW MY SHIRT WAS YELLOW BUT LOOKED TURQUOISE -BY THE WAY-NO BLOOD...

that was lucky. On Friday during the football game Kaye + I went to smoke a joint and Kaye had some resin on her lip so I gave her a Kleenex. She kept wiping + wiping + resin kept coming off I wiped my mouth and I had it too. We were freaking out til we notice the resin was really yellow flowers on the Kleenex.

Did you hear that O'Bannion's brother got expelled last week and when he was in the principals office he slipped Mr. Irvine some acid?

SO THAT'S WHY HE WAS GONE FOR 4 DAYS. LISTEN TO THIS - DON + I GOT IN A WRECK IN THE PARKING LOT AT SCHOOL. WE HAD JUST COME BACK FROM SCORING A POUND. WE PANICKED CUZ THE COPS WERE ON THEIR WAY. DON WAS RUNNING ACROSS THE PARKING LOT WITH THE PAPER BAG + MS. STROUD SAW HIM ·SHE KNEW....

No Way! Did you see Darla + Simone after lunch. It was Simone's B·Day-They each drank six beers. Came back to school + immediately threw up - sprayed "Charlie" on + went straight to class.

You are crazy. I heard Don got caught under your bed

NO HE DIDN'T GET CAUGHT. MY DAD CAME IN AND ASKED ME WHY I WAS SWEATING, I GO "GOD, DAD"

THAT'S HILARIOUS. MICHELLE FLIPPED HER PARENTS STATION WAGON CUZ SHE WAS SO LUDED OUT OF HER MIND. SHES OK· THANK GOD

Is this class boring or what

HELPFUL HINTS BY BENNY

WHAT TO DO WHEN YOU HAVE A SUBSTITUTE TEACHER

(Always realize that, because the substitute is eager for acceptance and doesn't really know anyone or the deal, the element of surprise and the power of suggestion can be used to your youthful, highly impressionable and inquisitive advantage.)

1. Commit to mispronouncing your substitute's name as often as possible.

2. Change your name.

3. Skip! Have someone sign your name when the sheet is passed — better known as a "paid vacation."

4. Hide all the books, chalk, pencils, and pens.

5. Tell them that you have acute asthma, and you have to go outside every ten minutes to breathe.

6. Misspell most words (hopefully on the backboard).

7. Fake a seizure! It's always good for a scare and usually a free ride to the clinic.

8. Laugh at everything being said/taught. At first the temp thinks the class is easily amused, after about fifteen minutes the nervous perspiration/frustration starts wearing them down.

9. After a majority vote, demand filmstrips in the name of democracy. Particularly effective with substitute American History and Social Studies teachers.

WHAT'S IN PICKFORD'S LOCKER?

1. Two photos of Michelle.
2. Box of baggies with one containing "sandwich fixins."
3. Job™ 1.25's pinched closed by a plumed alligator clip.
4. Emergency cigarette in corked test tube (a Viceroy™.)
5. Immaculate Uncle Henry Buck knife and accompanying leopard-skin sheath.
6. A Slinky™
7. Faded rebel flag head band.
8. Black and white striped wide tooth hip comb affectionately dubbed "Pepe le Pew."
9. A mirror
10. Pop rocks™

Bally FIREBALL

Pinball Flippers and Kickers and other helpful hints

by Ron Slater

Pinball is about the coolest sport around that's legal today, and even though the movie "Tommy" made it a fad, it still hasn't been ruined... One thing that pinball has going for it is that it keeps getting faster and better. Yeah, I know some of you like air hockey, but it just doesn't give you that cool, grooving feeling you get when you get an extra game and hear that "klop" behind the back glass of your favorite pinball machine. Here's some pinball knowledge for you to check out next time you've got a quarter and a friend to play against.

Probably the most important thing is that the flippers are different from one table to the next. Williams' machines by far have the fastest, like "Gulfstream." You'll hit more glass on Williams' tables than any other kind. Then you've got the machines made by Bally, whose flippers

aren't as fast but are really reliable. And last (and definitely least) is Gottlieb, whose flippers are so weak that sometimes they barely work. Even when they do work, you better push that button a hair-splitting second early because they are slooow!!

PLAY

continued page 121

Tips On How To Play The Fireball

1. There's no special on Fireball so the name of the game is pure points.

2. Don't start off by pulling the plunger all the way back (3/4 is a good bet). Try to get the ball to drop in the middle lanes, near the top of the table, because that's where the high scoring points are located.

3. Shoot for the sockets on the left and right. These holes trap your ball and then the machine will give you another ball. Then try to hit the yellow "Release Odin" or "Release Wotan" bumpers or the lane that says "Release the Fire Gods." There's a trapped ball in there that rolls up and hits a yellow target and then both trapped balls are in play at the same time.

4. When more than one ball is going, try to put one or two back in the sockets again. Although the machine never gives you more than three balls, it always helps to have a spare sitting in the hole.

5. When two or three balls are going at once, don't count on the closed flippers or the kicker or gate to stay on for you. It's too easy, with that many balls going, for these to turn on and off too fast to keep track of while you're juggling all those pinballs.

6. Practice.

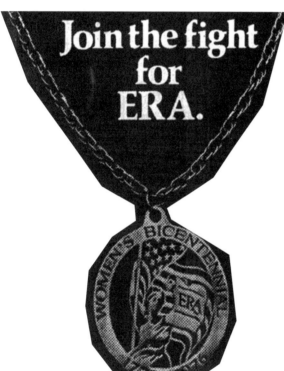

Kaye Faulkner

First sentence: "Leave me alone!"
Spoken as an overweening aunt pokes her in the cheek.

Leadership ability: Leads her classmates in unified stomping while their fifth grade teacher, the dreaded Miss Settergren, is out of the room. Tiles drop off the ceiling below and the whole class gets detention.

Consciousness lifters: After exhausting the various classics of girlish literature—Black Beauty, Nancy Drew, "True Romance" Comics, etc.—at triple speed, she encounters Harold Robbins' The Carpetbaggers at a church book sale. Convinced by Robbins that sex mainly consists of taking showers and smoking cigarettes, she gets a copy of Betty Friedan's The Feminine Mystique, figuring it may explain things. That same week, she sees John Lennon sing "Woman is the Nigger of the World" on The Mike Douglas Show. Consciousness soaring, she burns all her training bras in the backyard barbecue pit. Plunges into a paperback of Germaine Greer's The Female Eunuch given to her by her older sister.

Pet peeve: Girls who write with big loops and put little circles or hearts above the letter "i."

Gilligan's Island conspiracy theory: Is convinced that the Professor is keeping everyone on the island for some twisted experimentation; plans to cross breed Mary Ann and Gilligan to create a "Master simple race."

Wall hanging: Cross stitch embroidery which reads: "This too shall pass. Camp Nippersink 7/09/72".

Secret ambition: Wants to be an editor of a flashy New York magazine until Sylvia Plath's The Bell Jar convinces her that this is a bad idea. Currently considering a career as an author of subversive romance novels.

Currently reading: Fear of Flying by Erica Jong.

Favorite drink: Screwdriver.

FREEDOM · LIBERTY · EQUALITY · BROTHERHOOD · PREJUDICE · EXPLOITATION · WAR · RACISM ·

Kaye Faulkner
Ms. Stroud
5th Period: Social Studies

WHY WE NEED THE ERA

"I am Woman, hear me roar/
In numbers too big to ignore...
If I have to, I can do anything/
I am strong; I am invincible..."
—Helen Reddy, 1972

When I graduate from high school and enter college, studies have proven that I'll be discriminated against in the classroom. When I get a job, I won't be paid as much as a man holding the same position. There is only a slim chance that I'll get to the top of my profession; most likely I'll be making coffee for my male superiors. If I decide to be a housewife and mother, society won't value the work that I do as much as it will my husband's. If I become pregnant while I'm employed, instead of being allowed to take a leave of absence, I may be fired. In short, I am a second class citizen.

The Declaration of Independence declares that the citizens of the United States are guaranteed freedom and equality. Still, women, who comprise more than 50% of the population, have not enjoyed equal rights, but have lived under the unjust authority of men. These men, in their ignorance and greed for power, have come up with numerous arguments to deny women liberty. In the past, women were often not allowed to get an education, own land, or even be respected as full partners in marriage. They weren't allowed to practice law and were not permitted to vote until 1920. Amazingly enough, this obsolete sexism still affects us every day because, though the 14th Amendment guarantees that no state shall deny "to any person within its jurisdiction the equal protection of those laws," women living two hundred years after the signing of the Declaration of Independence are still not guaranteed protection from discrimination.

We need the Equal Rights Amendment. It simply states, "Equality of rights under the law shall not be denied or abridged by the United States or by any state on account of sex." In short, it will finally make discrimination illegal, and guarantee that men and women are treated equally. It will force lawmakers to change unfair existing laws and pre-vent discriminatory ones from being enacted. It will ensure that women receive equal opportunities and pay, and that they are viewed as equal partners in marriage, entitled to the same privileges and responsibilities. The ERA is endorsed by President Carter (as well as former Presidents Johnson, Nixon, and Ford), both the Democratic and Republican parties, the National Organization for Women, and many other organizations.

The status quo fights the passage of the ERA. Groups have formed especially to oppose it, arguing that it will weaken morals in this country, draft mothers during wartime, and force us to use co-ed bathrooms. The most well-known opponent of the ERA is Phyllis Schlafly, who claims that if the bill is passed, women will lose the right to be "provided with a home" or stay home to be a wife and mother if they choose. Recognize this opposing force for what it is: a display of pitiful cowardice and hypocrisy in the face of change. The ERA will change the law. It will give value to women's roles. It will not force men and women to change their personal dealings with one another.

The ERA has been stalled since 1948. Finally, in 1970, a petition to pass the amendment succeeded in the House of Representatives, but was defeated in the Senate. It must be ratified by three-fourths (38) of the states by March 22, 1979. So far, thirty-five states have ratified. If only three more states ratify the ERA, women in this country will finally receive the freedom and equality guaranteed them. Then we will all be first class citizens.

Ms. LIBERTY

MICHELLE
BURROUGHS

BIRTH SIGN: "Pisces, Virgo rising is a very good sign" Loggins and Messina burbled in "Danny's Song," and no one ever told Michelle they were wrong, so hearing it on the radio about a zillion times gave her confidence, negating the fact that it's really not so hot astrology-wise.

SLIGHT DRAWBACK: When she got a part-time job at an Orange Julius store, her older brother Bill kept calling her "a Pisces working for scale."

REVELATION: Attending the 1973 Watkins Glen rock festival in upstate New York with her older brother.

ROLE MODELS: Peggy Lipton's character on *The Mod Squad*, later Joni Mitchell, and Lily Tomlin in *Nashville*.

FAVORITE HALTER TOP: Red suede buckskin, so comfortable it reminds her of her boyfriend, Kevin Pickford.

FAVORITE ALBUM COVER: Syd Barrett's "The Madcap Laughs." Totally flipped out when Pickford explained how David Gilmour helped produce the work even after replacing the blithering Syd in his former group Pink Floyd; true artists.

BIGGEST WORRY: Pickford will get busted for selling pot and sent up the river.

FASHION FIRSTS: Gets a pair of Earth Shoes before anyone else, and a pair of photo-gray sunglasses that stay dark for a while indoors, making them perfect for hiding pot eyes.

TURN ON: When Kevin reads passages from Tolkien's The Simarillon while the two swing solemnly in a macramé hammock she crocheted.

INSPIRATIONAL VOLUME: Hermann Hesse's Siddhartha.

FAVORITE SONGS: Patti Smith's "Break It Up" and "Free Money" from Horses.

FANTASY ROLE: To play Alice in the musical stage version of "Go Ask Alice." As a rock opera, the main character Alice would come across as more multi-emotional and less hopeless. Wants to take artistic liberties by making her character a candle sculptress instead of a drug-gobbling simp... more frills less pills!

CHEEKO

Why do a Show about **Mexican-Americans** when there are **five** times as many **Puerto Ricans** in the U.S.?!?

Who needs **five** times as many **protest letters**?

Hey, Cheeko! How can you stand being with that miserable old man all the time?

I don't know! I guess it's because Egg Brawny is like a **Father** to me!

You mean it?!?

Sure! My **Old Man** was a cantankerous miserable slob who treated me rotten, **too!**

Can anyone explain why an **old bigot** like me took a **minority group kid** in as a partner?

NBC wanted a **controversial Show!**

What's the controversy in **THIS** Show?

Whether or not it's a **COMEDY!** By the way, can you fix my car?

How should I know? In 39 weeks, we haven't fixed **one!**

GARAGE

EGG BRAWNY PROP.

CHEEKO

FREDDIE

NAME: Freddie Prinze

BIRTH DATE: June 22, 1954

BIRTH PLACE:
New York, New York

HAIR: Brown

EYES: Brown

SIGN: Cancer

TV CHARACTER:
Chico Rodriguez on
Chico and the Man

HERITAGE: "Hungarican"
(Hungarian/Puerto-Rican)

CHILDHOOD: Grew up in the Spanish Ghetto area of Washington Heights in New York; his mother enrolled him in dance classes to help him take off excess weight, which didn't sit too well with the neighborhood kids, so he switched to karate.

HOW BE GOT INTO SHOWBIZ: Became a stand-up comedian in high school, graduated from New York's High School for the Performing Arts; before he knew it he was doing the club circuit, starting with Manhattan's Improv Club and first appeared on TV on *The Jack Paar Show*.

HOW HE GOT DISCOVERED: While performing on *The Johnny Carson Show*, he was spotted by producer Jimmie Komack, who cast him in *Chico and the Man*.

FAVORITE LINE: "Looking good"

BEST FRIEND: Tony Orlando, who is often mistaken for Freddie.

FATHERLY ADVISE HE GOT FROM JACK ALBERTSON ABOUT MARRIAGE: "There are no highs or lows— and no regrets. You just hang in there."

PAST PLAYTHING: ex-wife Katherine Cochran, Kitty Bruce, others too numerous to mention

RECENT PLAYTHING: Raquel Welch

ONLY THE LONELY

March, 1976

by Cynthia Dunn

Loneliness. Alienation. On the outside looking in. Not belonging to anyone or anything. Rejection. Many members of our student body never have the misfortune of experiencing any of these aspects. Their lives are full of friends and countless activities to fill their days. But then, there are those who suffer the above-mentioned aspects — the forgotten ones who go unnoticed among the countless faces of the student body. Maybe that's why the new movie TAXI DRIVER touched me so deeply because I can almost fully identify with the painful loneliness and isolation of the main character, Travis Bickle (who is brilliantly played by Robert De Niro, and who was also in GODFATHER II). In the movie, Travis is a solitary, almost child-like man without love, friends or family, and who almost continuously drives a cab in New York City. When he's not working, he spends countless hours at X-rated movie theaters, or within the cramped confines of his dingy, one-room apartment, where he pens his thoughts in a diary. Loneliness leads him to reach out to a beautiful — but stuck up-young woman named Betsy (played by Cybill Shepherd) who is working for a presidential candidate. But, Betsy dumps Travis when he innocently tries to take her to an X-rated movie on their first and only date. Something in Travis snaps — he begins to grow more and more psychotic, and he becomes obsessed with buying guns of all types and sizes. In his delusions, he believes he is some sort of "savior,"

continued page 122

AND THE HAM

DARLA MARKS

Role model: Barbara Stanwyck in Samuel Fuller's *Forty Guns*, seen on the Late Late Show while her parents are at a cocktail party and her sitter's busy making out. She is deeply, indelibly impressed by Stanwyck's portrayal of a "hard drivin' woman with a whip."

Success secrets: At 13, catches her mother kissing one of her father's junior employees. Uses this information to secure flexible curfew hours and a more generous clothing allowance.

Heroines: While other little girls pass the time with <u>Charlotte's Web</u> and *True Romance Comics*, Darla raids her mother's bookshelf and discovers <u>Miss Tallulah Bankhead</u> by Lee Israel, a biography of the brilliant, sexually insatiable actress of the forties and fifties.

Favorite song: "Dream On." (Steven Tyler has a better jaw and lip structure than Mick Jagger and Marc Bolan combined.)

Accomplishments: Masters Elizabeth Taylor's beauty secrets as reported in *Redbook.*

Sophomore year scandal: Seduces, then abandons star Quarterback Joe Huckabee, whose despair over losing her makes him blow several touchdown passes and ruins his chances for an athletic scholarship at the University of Oklahoma.

Beverage: Jack Daniels (in honor of Keith Richards) mixed with Coca-Cola.

Dream Dilemma: David Soul and Paul Michael Glaser asking her out at the same time on the same night; although keeping it a secret from the other would be almost impossible because they're partners.

Dream muscle: A taut tricep. It should look like the letter "R."

Dream angel: Kate Jackson hands down. No one runs in a flaxen pants suit with a .38 caliber like Sabrina.

Ambitions: Go national with *Go Ask Darla*; perhaps enter politics.

Typical dude diagram

Hair
Parted down the middle, feathered back with sideburns, long wild stoner hair or bangs swooshed over the forehead.

Necklace
Beads on leather string, pukka shells, chains and drug paraphernalia.

Shirts
T-shirts, sports jerseys, muscle shirts, concert t-shirts, dress shirt in polyester with big collars and very fitted body.

Belts
leather with a double row of holes, braided, tooled leather.

Jeans and Pants
Jeans: tight, tight tight and flared. First pick are Levi's or fancy jeans with designs down the outside of the leg. Other Options: painter pants, overalls, dress slacks in shiny knit.

Shoes
See Shoe News Now!

by Jodi Kramer

What a hunk and well dressed too!!!
Coolest look for a night out
cruising for chicks.

This macho sleazy look is great
for parties or pool halls

Bicentennial fashions are
sweeping the nation. We've waited
200 years to wear this much
red, white and blue.

In the Jr. High crowd, these casual styles are perfect for school,
street wear or a quick get away by these young studs

FOXY

By Jody Kramer

Look like a fox not a fiasco!!!! My best fashion advice on the do's and don'ts, ins and outs, of dressing for high school. The way life works you have to look cool to be popular so here are my suggestions:

Hair tips

For chicks, long and straight parted down the middle continues to be the biggest look. Of course your hair has to be absolutely straight. (tip: roll your hair on really huge oj cans or iron flat if you have the frizzies) the newer styles are the wedge like Dorothy Hamill or wings and layers like Farrah Fawcett, Lee Majors' wife who does the shampoo ads.

Tops

Your basic wardrobe should consist of tons of t-shirts, tank tops, tube tops, halter tops, vests, crop tops, crocheted pieces, all kinds of little shirts that are stretchy, short, tight or bare. These tops should be in a wide variety of colors and wear a matching belt with everything. If inflation is hitting you hard buy a rainbow colored belt and wear it a lot. Another thing about t-shirts is the little cap sleeve makes everyone's arms look fat, so don't worry about it just wear them because everyone else does.

There is nothing tackier than your bra hanging out of all these little bare tops, so buy the adjustable halter and strapless bras that are always uncomfortable or falling down. Or if you are not going to wear a bra at least wear band aids so your nips don't show - that is if you want a nice girl reputation.

With all the bare clothes you just have to be tan, so spend any chance you get laying out for hours soaked in baby oil and iodine. Don't try to the fake tan stuff, it will turn you orange and ruin your life, trust me!

Polyester blouses with large collars and cuffs are really cool. They come in great bright colors in this shiny, slippery fabric that never wrinkles. These look best accessorized with a thin gold chain with a heart or butterfly charm or a small scarf around your neck and your frosted, shimmery eyeshadow and gooiest lip gloss.

Jeans/pants

Jeans are the most critical item in your closet. It may seem superficial but if you don't wear jeans that look right forget ever going steady with a hunk. It's easy, tight from the waist to the thighs then flares to the floor (your shoes no not show, see shoe article on page —).

Designs that make your jeans more cool: patchwork denim patterns, frayed bottoms from dragging the ground, inset fabrics down the side seams, and jeans with two sets of zippers and no waist band.

Ditto jeans with the saddleback, that horseshoe shape around the butt are cute, too.

Other types of bottoms - of course your basic jeans are the best thing to wear but that can get boring so try to throw on something different like painters pants, overalls, a jumpsuit, or gauchos once a week.

Out: jeans that are baggy in the butt, panty lines and high waters.

(picture of high water striped pants with platforms)

Jewelry

Turquoise and silver jewelry with chunky stones are in, so is wearing your boyfriend's senior ring with lots of yarn tied around the back or on a string around your neck. Mood rings are cute. Most girls wear lots of rings, one necklace of beads or chains and small dangling earrings or studs.

Dressing up

Speaking of dresses, no one really wears them very often because them went from mini's to midi's to maxi's in a few years and now they are right at the knee and what fun is that. For special occasions you wear long hostess dresses and for the prom it is romantic long dresses flowing with ruffles and lace.

Do's:

...gooey lip gloss goes
with shiny fabrics

...this best dressed couple
is wearing polyester dress
shirts with ditto saddleback
jeans and Levi's.

...lots of rings
won't slow you
down, unless it's a
mood ring; beware
of the curious gray.

...the bathroom is ideal for taking
fashion inventory. Check early and
check often, sometimes a spotter is
necessary for the tougher clenched
buttocks lace-up calls.

...jeans with fabric
inset are happening

FASHION

GO?
Ask Darla

Help Me Please, Darla Dear

I ironed my hair straight as a board just like Cher told me to, but every time I think I look like a MILK DUD! I love ratted hair high as the sky, but it's just not as "fashionable" right now...Darla, I wanna be cool, what do I "hair" do?

Shartwilla Washington

Dear Flat in Topeka,

To heck with "fashion," be that Fabulous Hair Hopper that you want to be! Wear extra wiglets piled up high on top of each other, rat your hair up over a large coffee can or even swirl it around a beachball! Start your own Hairdo "World of Wonders"...bows, plastic flowers, and fuzzy bees can be pleasant accents, even a tiara for daytime wear will most surely get attention. The future of fashion can be anyone's idea! Rat on Baby!

Hairs to you, Darla

Darla Dish,

How 'bout that kissing-on-the-first-date question!

Annie Sprinkles
Love to Love

Well Miss Sprinkles...

Yes! Sure, it's OK. The girls I know kiss the guys even before they go out with them! Formality is gone, casual is in! Uptight is out, relaxed is the manner. "Kissing a boy good night is not considered sex," I say. "Sex is considered sex."

Say Babe:

I guess you don't get many letters very often from men but I just wanted to say how we guys think it's totally OK for women to go bare breasted topless at public swimming areas. For that matter, we wouldn't even mind if they went bottomless too! Ha-Ha, bet you won't print this!

Orville Bunt

Dear Dumb Bubba:

Yes, I will print it just to give me the excuse to write:

"DIE SEXIST PIG"

in huge letters in my column. Please take a hint, human garbage.

Disgusted Darla

Darla:

Since I've been born, it seems like there's always been fighting all over the world. My father told me his life was full of war, the same as his father's was. Is there anything that we, the youth of not only America but the world can do to stop this chain of heartbreak and pain? There has to be more from our generation than a legacy of destruction, don't you think?

Candice Matthews

Thank you,

Thank you Candice for making us all realize that life is more than just football games, proms, and Dairy Queen cruising. They say we're the most informed and aware generation in history. I say let's challenge ourselves to use that knowledge to further the good of humankind. Start by changing yourself; and them those around you. Candice, I'd vote for you for president!

Love, Darla

Too Crazy For Love?

Dear Darla:

I have been reading your column for several issues now and I think it's really great what you are doing for people with problems. I only hope that you can help me with mine. I am 16 years old and sort of depressed. Yet I don't know where my head is at. On weekends I go to bars and sometimes meet guys. Many of my girlfriends feel that I am too young but my reason for this is I want to find someone that really cares about me, and the guys in school are bent. I met this one guy I really dug. He was 19 and we got along good. The only problem was he was in a band and was into his music too much. Well I am not seeing him anymore. I wish you could help me think of ways to meet guys. I don't really have trouble meeting them, it is just holding on to them. Sometimes I get too stoned and start talking crazy to my girl-

70

friends, which freaks and turns off the guys we meet. I tried to calm myself but it doesn't work—it gets deeper and deeper. I love being crazy and just having a pisser, but I also would like to have a guy. What can I do?

Loser Yet Lover

Dear Loser Yet Lover:

It seems, at least, you're on the right track. Guys in rock bands like to get stoned, and there's something you have in common, already. In fact, most guys in rock bands are crazy too. I think you'd be actually lucky to find someone who's crazier. Just be patient, Robert Plant wasn't married in a day!

Pot and Ruination

Dear Darla:

I'm a seventeen year old boy. I've got a problem I need desperate help with. My problem is pot smoking. I've already talked to my mother about it and she has tried her best but failed. I've tried to quit but I find it extremely hard when all my friends and neighbors turn-on. I've tried to turn them down but I'm fighting a losing battle. They talk me into it every single time. I can't just change friends like my mother suggests. Please print this so I can find out what to do. I need HELP. I'm afraid to see what will happen if it goes on any longer. Thanks so very, very much!

Frightened

Dear Frightened:

At this point the problem and the desperation is not primarily the pot or the bad reactions you didn't mention, or the fact that all your friends and neighbors urge you to turn on. Getting new friends isn't the problem either. The problem is how you come on to yourself.

I would like to ask you a question. Could someone like a friend or neighbor talk you into jumping off a bridge, or shooting someone, or wearing a dress in public? Why not? Because it would be bad for you? Yet, some people do these things. Some people smoke pot, too, and others don't. Some who smoke have simple pleasant reactions, and others, like yourself, have psychotic reactions that really screw them up. So.... jump off that bridge if you want too. Run naked, wear a dress, but if you do, it should always be your own decision.

Deathly Dreamer

Dear Darla:

I am female and 17. I would like to know if I am going insane. Ever since I was six, I have been living in a dream world which has been becoming more real than life in the last few months. I am also developing a feeling that I'm repulsive and hateful to other people and they go out of their way to hurt me. I can't stand to see myself in mirrors and go out of my way to avoid them and people. I am a compulsive liar and failure. The thing that frightens me most, besides the loss of reality, is these constant death wish feelings and I am afraid that I may kill myself in the near future.

Please excuse my cowardice in not signing my name and address but mental illness is not acceptable in my family and there is no way they'll let me go to a psychiatrist. So please help me.

Sincerely,
Needs Help Bad

Dear Needs Help Bad:

Sometimes when I stress out, I like to take in a movie, because there tends to be some hidden lesson mixed in with all the Hollywood Glamour. Try checking out The Omen, Sybil, One Flew Over the Cuckoo's Nest, and then kick back and try to compare it with what's bothering you. You're only 17, and you have a lot of years ahead of you, and it just doesn't pay to be paranoid .

It's all relative,
Darla

Darla,

Since I don't have very much money at any one time, I find it extremely difficult to be able to afford to go on dates to cool places. Sharlene, my girl-friend, insists she helps pay for part of the evening. What do I do? I feel unmanly and am embarrassed at the thought of her having to pay?

Donnie No Dough

Dear Penniless,

A major step in battling inflation is an alternative that some teenage girls may have regarded as unthinkable just a few years ago: paying for part of the date themselves! Maybe some boys will be insulted if girls offer to pay. But if you insist, they'll usually agree. In this time of troubled money, we must all do our part equally.

Dutch treat should be a breeze,

Darla

NAME: Farrah Fawcett-Majors

BIRTH DATE: Feb. 2, 1946

BIRTH PLACE: Corpus Christi, Texas

HAIR: Blonde

EYES: Green

SIGN: Aquarius

ANCESTRY: French-Indian. "I'm one-eighth Choctaw Indian. I was going to say Cherokee—it's so much more glamorous."

TV CHARACTER: Jill Munroe on *Charlie's Angels*

COLLEGE LIFE: At the University of Texas at Austin she discovered that she had a great gift as an artist and sculptress.

FIRST BIG BREAK AT FAME: While a frosh at UT, she was chosen one of the "Ten Most Beautiful Coeds." A Hollywood publicist spotted her pic in a newspaper and invited her to Tinsel Town. Soon she was signed by Screen Gems, earning $350 a week.

BIG LOVE: Her hubby, Lee Majors

REBEL YELL NEWS
COMEDY TONIGHT
May 23, 1977

By Don Dawson

Seeing that the staff of our illustrious school paper wouldn't know a good joke if it bit them (well, you-know-where), I've come up with a list of my favorite comedy records. I use the term "record" loosely. Some of the bits from my favorites are best seen on T.V. or in concert movies. So here is my list...Questions or comments are best kept to yourself. See you in the funny papers.

1. Richard Pryor's records, TV., or movies: He's the funniest human alive, maybe ever.

2. Monty Python's Flying Circus: I hear more people trying to do these guys' jokes than any other comic or troupe. Their T.V. shows and the Holy Grail movie will be funny forever.

3. George Carlin: Words are funny. Especially, the seven you can't say on T.V.

4. Rodney Dangerfield: Shut up! I love this guy.

5. Lily Tomlin: Geraldine, need I say more?

6. Saturday Night Live: I'm not exactly sure what's going on, but I'm pretty sure that it's hilarious.

Honorable mentions:

Cheech and Chong, "Dave's Not Here"

National Lampoon, "I'm a Woman"

Robert Klein, "No Talking During a Nuclear Holocaust"

Martin Mull, "Dueling Tubas"

Melvin Spivey's Top 10

SPECIAL TO THE REBEL YELL

Melvin Spivey's Top 10

May 14, 1976

There's a riot going on at the "Rebel Yell". Hey y'all Melvin Spivey says "Don't forget that party connection this summer... say it loud 'I'm down and I'm proud!'". The funk will get you if the soul don't blow your mind this time. These are my ten heavy heavy rotation grooves. Remember, just because a record has a groove don't mean it's in the groove. Peace and we gone.

1. **Parliament**
   "Tear the Roof Off the Sucker (Give up the Funk)"
2. **Lou Rawls "You'll Never Find Another Love Like Mine"**
3. **Leon Haywood "Strokin" (pt.11)**
4. **Sylvers "Boogie Fever"**
5. **Ohio Players "Fopp"**
6. **Diana Ross "Love Hangover"**
7. **Willie, Hutch "Party Down"**
8. **Earth, Wind, and Fire "Can't Hide Love"**
9. **Silver Convention "Get Up and Boogie"**

RUNNER UP UP UPS

Kool and the Gang "Open Sesame-Part I"

Spinners "Rubber Band Man"

Stevie Wonder "I Wish"

Wild Cherry "Play That Funky Music"

Dr. Buzzard's Original Savannah Band
   "Whispering/Cherchez La Femme/Se Si Bon"

Brick "Dazz"

James Brown "Get Up Offa That Thing"

NAME: Lee Majors

BIRTH DATE: April 23, 1940

BIRTH PLACE: Wyandotte, Michigan

HAIR: Brown

EYES: Blue

SIGN: Taurus

TV CHARACTER: Col. Steve Austin—
The Six Million Dollar Man

BOYHOOD HERO: James Dean

COLLEGE DAYS: Got an education
degree from Eastern Kentucky State

WHY HE GOT INTO SHOWBIZ:
As recreation director for the Los
Angeles Department of Parks and
Recreation he met a lot of actors and
show people who encouraged him to
give acting a try.

HIS FIRST BREAK: The late James
Dean's former agent, Dick Clayton,
got him into the MGM studio drama
school, which led to his role on The
Big Valley in 1965.

FARRAH FANTASY:
Would like her by his side
night and day.

A ROCK'N'ROLL TRIVIA QUIZ

1. Bob Dylan's white face tour.
a. Bob and Carol and Ted and Alice
b. Rolling Joints Revue
c. Rolling Thunder Revue
d. Dinosaurs of Rock Revue

2. Who will "show you the way" with this double live LP?
a. Chicago
b. Rocky
c. Peter Frampton
d. Edgar Winter

3. Led Zeppelin...
a. had their own jet for tours.
b. slept with fifteen year olds.
c. broke attendance records.
d. all of the above.

4. Who is the "Joker, Toker, Midnight Stroker"?
a. Stephen Stills
b. Leo Sayer
c. Steve Miller
d. Gary Wright

5. Emerson Lake and Palmer's triple live LP.
a. Welcome Back Kotter
b. Welcome back my friends to the show that never ends, Ladies and Gentlemen...
c. Thanks For Nothin'
d. The Sonny and Cher Show

6. The Eagles album that contained three Top Ten hits.
a. Lyin' Eyes
b. One Of These Days Alice
c. Take It To The Limit
d. One Of These Nights

7. John Denver...
a. loves Mary Jane.
b. is a religious fanatic.
c. thinks LA.. is his lady.
d. thanked god he was a country boy.

8. The Number One Hit "Tie A Yellow Ribbon" was performed by.
a. Sonny
b. Dawn
c. Cher
d. Rufus

9. 461 Ocean Blvd. was...
a. Eric Clapton's #1 hit album.
b. down the road a piece.
c. Bob Marley's house.
d. your mom's house.

10. Who won the Grammy Award for Record of the Year for 1975?
a. Pink Floyd
b. Paul Simon
c. Captain and Tennille
d. Led Zeppelin

11. Keith Relf, an original member of the legendary Yardbirds, died from...
a. the shame of not sticking with Jimmy Page.
b. electrocution.
c. disco.
d. boredom.

12. Frank Zappa warned us...
a. don't play records backwards.
b. don't cross in the middle of the block.
c. don't eat the yellow snow.
d. don't talk back.

13. "Why Can't We Be Friends" is?
a. A good idea.
b. Wars' 1975 hit.
c. Jimmy Carter's slogan.
d. The title of Gerald Fords' autobiography.

14. British teen idols The Bay City Rollers first gold single was
a. Saturday Night
b. Theme from Swat
c. I Love Music
d. Junk Food Junkie

15. Most people agree that Donna Summer had this many orgasms on her disco hit "Love to Love You Baby"
a. 13
b. 7
c. 1 (a big one)
d. 30

16. Jimmy Carter...
a. quoted Bob Dylan.
b. listened to Led Zeppelin.
c. cheated in his heart.
d. all of the above.

ONE MILLIONTH U.S. MARRIAGE DESTROYED BY WOMEN'S LIBERATION MOVEMENT 1975
5c U.S. POSTAGE

TENTH ANNIVERSARY OF THE 1965 1975 8c EAST COAST POWER BLACKOUT

1,000th "LUCY" SHOW RE-RUN in Wichita, Kansas August 30, 1975
WALDO DIRNDL champion viewer
30c

17. "Bohemian Rhapsody" is a 6 minute sleeper hit by this band.
a. Supertramp
b. The Outlaws
c. Henry Gross
d. Queen

18. Fleetwood Mac's eponymous hit album contains this hit single
a. Evil Woman
b. Ding Dong the Witch is Dead
c. Rhiannon
d. Glinda

19. Jethro Tull's Ian Anderson plays the...
a. lyre.
b. flute.
c. bongos.
d. mouth harp.

20. "Shining Star" was their number one hit
a. The Ohio Players
b. Earth, Wind and Fire
c. The Starland Vocal Band
d. Rhythm Heritage

21. Steely Dan warned Rikki...
a. don't lose that number.
b. don't smoke!
c. don't cross in the middle of the block.
d. don't forget to brush.

22. Kiss' Gene Simmons is known for his...
a. fire breathing.
b. long tongue.
c. his panty collection.
d. all of the above.

23. Gary Wright had hits with "Dream Weaver" and "Love Is Alive" after leaving this band to go solo:
a. Humble Pie
b. Stealer's Wheel
c. Spooky Tooth
d. Jethro Tull

24. Bachman Turner Overdrive's stuttering number one hit.
a. "You Ain't Seen Nothin' Yet"
b. "We're An American Band"
c. "Take Me To The River"
d. "Boogie Down"

25. Led Zeppelin launched their label Swan Song with this million seller band:
a. Roxy Music
b. Heart
c. Bad Co.
d. Ambrosia

26. Lynyrd Skynyrd gave Led Zeppelin's "Stairway To Heaven" a run for money with this FM hit
a. Freegarbage
b. Freebird
c. Freemoney
d. Free your mind

SPIRO T. AGNEW MEMORIAL
Becoming a household word 1c
SPIRO T. AGNEW MEMORIAL
Denouncing the press 2c
SPIRO T. AGNEW MEMORIAL
Blaming the intellectuals 3c
SPIRO T. AGNEW MEMORIAL
Getting the axe 4c

27. Grand Funk's comeback hit declares...
a. We're Not Dead Yet
b. We Were Lost, But Now We're Not
c. We're An American Band
d. We're Learning to Play Now

28. Bowie's redheaded stage persona that he took home at night:
a. Freddy Mercury
b. Reg Dwight
c. Gary Glitter
d. Ziggy Stardust

29. Considered the first Punk band:
a. Sex Pistols
b. The Ramones
c. Blondie
d. X

30. What is the title of the Bee Gees album containing the hits "Jive Talkin'" and "Nights on Broadway?"
a. Main Event
b. Gratitude
c. Main Course
d. Changesone

see answers page 122

AMERICA'S GROUPIES HONORING
LED ZEPPELIN FANATIC AVA GRUNDLEMAN
5c

COMMEMORATING THE FIRST POLLUTION OF LAKE ERIE
11c 1955

The AMERICAN Credo
I am not a crook RMNixon
2c UNITED STATES POSTAGE

CELEBRATING 50 YEARS OF PLANNED OBSOLESCENCE
2c

TENTH ANNIVERSARY OF WIFE SWAPPING
1965 1975
AL & TINA, BEN & RHONDA OF YOUNGSTOWN, OHIO

A&P CRUSHES 5,000th INDEPENDENT GROCER
24c 19c

10th ANNIVERSARY OF FERTILITY DRUGS
MR. & MRS. A. H. TINENAGON WITH ALBERT, BERNICE, CLAUDE, DONALD, EDGAR, FRANCINE, GRACE, HECTOR AND IMOGENE
5c

Fred O'Bannion

Boyhood heroes: Chuck Connors as The Rifleman, General George S. Patton as portrayed by George C. Scott, and the Incredible Hulk.

Boyhood hobbies: Stomping kids who are smaller than him, which most are, and blowing up G.I. Joe dolls with firecrackers.

Religious experience as a child: Seeing Detroit Lions defensive lineman Alex Karras cut down running backs like they were dandelions and generally leave devastation in his wake.

Teenage trauma: His dad pulverizing an antique chair in his frustration over ABC's pre-empting the sudden death overtime of the 1968 Jets playoff game for a new T.V. version of Heidi.

Favorite album: He tells everybody it's the Who's Quadrophenia, yet feels strangely stirred by a chance hearing of Mott the Hoople's "All the Young Dudes," a song about the joy of boyish glamour. He buys the Hoople record and hides it under his bed.

Junior year scandal: Streaks through the parking lot before school one morning. Nobody notices because at that very moment Ron Slater spectacularly crashes his mother's car into a telephone pole.

Motto: "Yea, though I walk through the valley of the shadow of death, I will fear no evil, for I am the meanest son of a bitch in the valley," taken from a popular wall poster.

Favorite potato chip: Funyun™.

Ambition: Considering a career in law enforcement as a sherriff. Not only is the gun and hat a major plus, but the sheriff gets to wear the star.

Favorite weasel: Angel on "The Rockford Files."

The Lighter Side of Grooming...

HOW TO KEEP THAT OLD L.P. PLAYING LONG.

by Melvin Spivey

The party's over but that doesn't mean that your records have to be. You've battered the best, now save the rest. Believe it or not, a badly damaged record full of dust, smeared with mustard, or drenched in soda pop can be washed clean! Now don't try tossing the latest Rod Stewart LP into the washing machine, because the chances are that even with a non—polluting detergent it will ruin your album. However, there's a little known method to save your disk when all else has failed.

First, prepare a clean, lint free drying cloth by spreading it out on a clean table. Then prepare a washing solution by using two drops of detergent to each pint of clean, warm water-not warmer then 90* F. Stand the record in a basin, leaning it on its edge. Wash the record using a clean cellulose sponge. Rotate the record until the entire surface has been washed several times. Always cleaning the direction of the grooves, never across. Repeat the entire procedure for the reverse side of the record. Then shake off as much excess water as possible and lay the record on one end of the drying cloth. Fold the other end over the record and dab gently until it's dry.

Here's some more helpful hints to help keep the good times rollin' and the LP's playin' long:

1. A ruined LP can be washed like a pair of dirty socks, but disc-washing should be saved as an emergency way to cure a sick LP.

2. A stylus is less than 0.00025 of an inch thick and has to trace thousands of miles of twisting grooves.

3. Although most turntables have a built-in stacking device, and album plopping on top of another causes scratches, screeches, an knicks.

4. Never touch the surface of a record! Invisible finger grease ruins more LP's than any other cause.

5. Always save the seemingly pointless inner-sleeve. The paper helps retain the shelf life of vinyl against carboard particle damage.

6. The sun wilts more than flowers, my friend. Watch that simmering back dash or <u>everybody's</u> gonna' sound like Black Sabbath.

7. Careful when cleaning dope on double albums. Lost seeds can wedge in-between discs and wreak havoc on grooves.

8. Mind that pets/pet hair steer clear of record collection. Covers and contents make great chew toys and scratching posts.

9. An LP is not a frisbee! That's <u>L</u>ong <u>P</u>laying, not Launching Pad.

Cool Wheelz!

Grey Ghost

O'Bannion "Grey Ghost"

MAKE: 1972 Plymouth Duster

DRIVEN BY: O'Bannion

ACQUIRED BY: An older cousin who tried to make it look like a race car

ENGINE: V-8 340 cubic inches

BORE AND STROKE: 4.04 V3.31

COMPRESSION RATIO: 10.5:1

HORSEPOWER:
275 BHP c 5000 rpm

CARBURETOR:
Carter type AV5 4 barrel

WHEELS: Cragar SS

HOOD SCOOP: Fake

CLUTCH: Burned-up

EXHAUST ACCESSORIES:
Ridiculous "Cherry Bomb" glass-pack mufflers

COLOR: Primer grey (project car)

8-TRACK: Got ripped-off

DRY WEIGHT: 3300 lbs

WET WEIGHT
(with trunk full of beer and ice): 3425 lbs

GLOVE COMPARTMENT CONTENTS:
Bottle rockets, M-80s, extra paddles, bottle of Wild Turkey

LAST TICKET RECEIVED:
Throwing explosives from a moving vehicle

BUMPER STICKER:
"America: Love It or Leave It"

HANGING FROM REAR-VIEW MIRROR:
A Playboy Bunny air freshener

TAKE IT WITH A GRAIN OF SALT WHEN...

...the President pardons the man who appointed him to the job, and then claims there was no deal.

...you're too fried to make a fist. It's a beautiful world!

...the President assures us that we can beat inflation by wearing a "WIN" button.

MELVIN SPIVEY

DILEMMA: Melvin lives in the spaces between the white suburban world of his schoolmates, and the black middle class world of his parents (Bill Cosby comedy albums, white fashion with Afro touches, subscription to Ebony).

ATTITUDE BOOGIE: Gets along okay with the cooler white boys at R.E. Lee since he grew up with one foot in their world, though he can't help feeling a little sorry for them when they betray their latent fear of black males. Doesn't hold it against them too much, though he's not above exploiting it for purposes of sport.

BOYHOOD HEROES: Willie Mays, Smokey Robinson.

WAKE-UP CALL: Watching the police on TV rain fire into the house where Symbionese Liberation Army leader Cinque—Patty Hearst's kidnapper—is holed up, he realizes what it means when white society gets seriously ticked off at a brother.

CURRENTLY ADMIRES: George Clinton, leader of Parliafunkadelicment Thang, i.e., the Stravinsky of post-psychedelic/pre-interstellar dance music. Melvin adorns his wall with a full-color poster of Clinton waterskiing on two dolphins while wearing a white shag Stetson, cowboy shirt, boots, white shag chaps and 100-watt grin.

RECENT ACCOMPLISHMENT: Introduces nine-ball and rotation to the poolroom at the Emporium, games that are beyond most of the other players. Increases his nightly winnings by $15-25.

MANIFESTO: Ishmael Reed's <u>Mumbo-Jumbo</u>, the Great Afro-American Novel about Papa LaBas, a hoodoo detective who gets involved in the age old battle between European and African culture.

BUMPERSTICKER: "Think! It ain't illegal yet!"

ANTHEMS: Isley's Brothers "Fight The Power" and the Ohio Players' "Love Rollercoaster."

TREE THE TIGERS

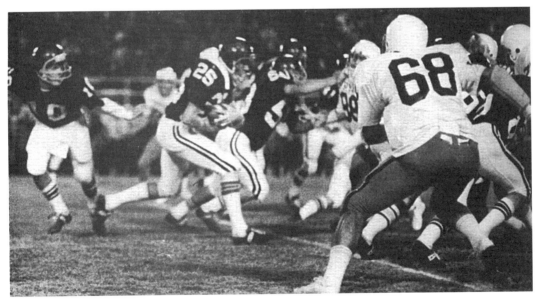

Our Number 68—Melvin Spivey—prepares to put a Tiger in his tank!

Mitch Kramer

Going with the flow:
Eleven-year-old Mitch wins the local Soap Box Derby when a combination of sweat and excess Brylcreem™ cloud the vision of the lead driver.

First model set: Rat Fink.

Favorite childhood after-school T.V. show
Dark Shadows.

Ideal girlfriend:
Jodie Foster in Candleshoe.

Secret fantasy:
Shavonne Wright (ever since she joined his older sister Jodi on a family trip to the beach when he was in 6th grade).

All time fantasy:
Raquel Welch in One Million Years B.C.

Advantage of having older sister:
Informs you what the "cool guys" wear, say and do ("Give them a subtle wink after you kiss them goodnight.")

Disadvantage of having older sister:
Those same "cool" guys want to beat your ass simply because you're her little brother.

Favorite movie:
2001: A Space Odyssey.

Favorite movie genre:
Though unnamed, all those "humans are expendable" provocations such as The Omega Man, The Andromeda Strain, Planet of the Apes (1st version only), and Soylent Green.

Crucial Musical Moment:
Totally "getting" the genius of Jethro Tull's "A Passion Play."

Recent reads:
"The True Believer" by Eric Hoffer and "Bo: Pitching and Wooing" by Bo Belinsky.

All time favorite:
Stranger in a Strange Land by Robert Heinlein.

Perennial baseball heroes:
Pete Rose, Bob Gibson.

Current Fave:
Mark "The Bird" Fydrich.

Quickly accelerating musical taste:
Started off 8th grade carting his Bread's Greatest Hits album to the weekly parties; ended up the year with Skynyrd, Zeppelin, and Aerosmith.

TELLY SAVALAS
BIRTH DATE: January 21, 1925
BIRTH PLACE:
Garden City, New York
HAIR: None (on his head)
EYES: Blue
SIGN: Aquarius
TV CHARACTER:
Lt. Theo Kojak on Kojak
FAVORITE LINE:
"Who loves you baby?"
PAST LIVES: GI in World War II (he got the Purple Heart); worked in field of psychology; executive director of State Department; senior director of news and special events for ABC-TV.
FAMOUS RELATIVES:
His mom Christina, who is an artist

FIRST MOVIE ROLE: Feto Gomez in Birdman of Alcatraz, for which he won an Oscar nomination.
HOW HE BROKE INTO SHOWBIZ AS AN ACTOR: On a whim he auditioned for a part in TV production of "Bring Home a Baby" that required a particular foreign accent: He got it.
OTHER ACHIEVEMENTS:
Won an Emmy in 1974 for Kojak
LEAST FAVORITE ROCK BAND:
Led Zeppelin— he and the band fought for the attention of photographers at London's Heathrow Airport.
PLAYTHING:
His wife Sally

April 23, 1976

Dear David

Man I wished you hadn't moved, so you could have cruized around with us last weekend. Well you know how it goes, but last weekend was wild! We drove to see Nugent at the Summit. Slater, Don, Shavonne, Wooderson, Pink and I rolled up about 20 joints, piled into the Camaro and went to the show. We found our seats and promply started to smoke all our joints. We had happenin seats man, right down front! The back up band came on stage with a big joint in his mouth. Then he threw a handful of pills into the audience and said, "Here you hungry dogs."

After a while we all got thirsty so I decided to make a beer run with Shavonne. We made it to the beer stand in our reefer haze and I got 6 large beers. But man, as soon as I bought the beers I started to feel faint. I asked Shavonne if she could hold the beers for a sec... I passed her the beers and then I passed out. I awoke shortly after that with a crowd of people staring down at me with Shavonne looking pretty fried out herself. Anyway I got my balance again, grabbed the beers and we lumbered back to our seats.

Fuck man, shortly after that I felt faint again. I handed her the beers and the scene played a rerun. An usher stuck his flashlight in my face and asked if I needed medical attention. I told him no, I was resting. Somehow we made it back to our seats with the beers intact. I decide not to smoke anymore pot that night. Just as Nugent swung down on a vine from his amps Slater got thirsty, collected more money, and went for beer. He never came back. Typical.

After the concert we saw Slater sitting alone and asked him what happened. He said, "You'll never believe what happened man— as soon as I got the beers I fainted and dropped all the beers on the floor. That's why I'm wet. Sorry man. By that time I didn't care and strangely enough felt totally sober. I thought maybe the pot had been sprayed with paraquat. I decided to buy this badass Nugent T-shirt and we all headed back to the cars. When we got there the camaro wasn't there. So Pink goes to find us a ride. While we're waiting for him a car full of red necks drive up. A guy jumped out and started to walk over in our direction. I thought to myself this guy is going to try and steal my T-shirt. Suddenly he threw a punch at me which I dodged and instead it hit Shavonne in the shoulder. Good thing she's tough... then I returned fire right on his nose. Then he pulled a knife and hit me with it's handle on my hand while simultaneously pulling on my t-shirt. There was a long line of traffic backed up leaving the show ---

People were hanging out their cars screaming "Kill him, kill him!" and stuff like do you want a club -- Our scramble continued and I held tight to my t-shirt. He finally ran off. What a trip. Pink eventually came back with some girls he meet and they took us home. So the next day at school I wore me Nugent shirt proudly but noticed it was full of holes. Knife holes man - geez. Geez whatta night, you should have been there, it rocked... I hear Areosmith is touring this summer, maybe you can come down and jam out with us... let me know man...

Keep on space truckin,

Kyle

THE AMERICAN DREAM

January, 1976

by Cynthia Dunn

Last week, a couple of my friends, and I went to see the new Robert Altman movie *NASHVILLE* , which I thoroughly enjoyed (although it is a bit long—a little over 2 & 1/2 hours). When the movie was over Don Dawson said, "I don't get it. This movie has too many things happening at once, and just exactly what is it all about, anyway?" I thought about Don's comment to myself, and realized, "He's right, in a way. What is this movie really about?" So, I decided that on the surface, *NASHVILLE* is a funny satire of the country music industry, and it stars Henry Gibson and Lily Tomlin (both from the now-defunct *Laugh-In* TV show), Karen Black (from *FIVE EASY PIECES* and *THE DAY OF THE LOCUST*), as well as a host of little known actors and actresses. The movie takes place over a five day period in Nashville, and concerns the intertwining lives of about 20 or so characters — some who are country music stars, and those who want to be stars. Then it occurred to me — this movie is really about the American dream in our society, today, and a lot of the characters in the movie embody the highs and lows of this cultural notion. I imagine there are a lot of you in the student body who don't believe that the American dream still exists — that it's one of those old fashioned notions that disappeared with our parents' generation. But, believe me, the

continued page 122

Special to the Rebel Yell

The First Anniversary of Saigon's Fall

April 30, 1976

• •

By Mike Newhouse

Departing Vietnam

Like many transfer students, Lien Nguyen Hall seemed quiet and shy when she started school last September. For her, the pressure of facing a new school, filled with unfamiliar faces, also reminded her of the fact that she faced a new country and a new culture.

Always polite to everyone, she never hinted at the terrible things that she experienced as she tried to get from Vietnam to the United States.

Lien knew some English from growing up in Da Nang, where thousands of Americans were based since the Vietnam war began escalating in 1965. She has made excellent progress in the last nine months.

Exactly one year after the last American left Saigon on April 30, 1975, Lien told Ms. Stroud's American History class what it was like when the last Americans left Vietnam.

"It was chaos, people would do anything to get out," Lien said.

"Everybody was so desperate. So many people worked for Americans: they so much wanted to leave because they knew the North Vietnamese would not forgive them. When I close my eyes, I

A map of Southeast Asia showing the movement of refugees south towards Saigon.

©1976 Courtesy of *Encyclopedia Brittanica, Inc.*

CHER BONO

BIRTH DATE: May 20, 1946

BIRTH PLACE: El Centro, CA

HAIR: Brunette

EYES: Brown

SIGN: Taurus

BAD CHILDHOOD EXPERIENCES: Didn't like her father (still doesn't); at age 14 took four Benzedrine, was up for an entire weekend.

GOOD CHILDHOOD EXPERIENCES: First had sex at age 14

HER TATTOOS: A butterfly and two roses on her derriere

WHY THEIR MARRIAGE FAILED: "One of the biggest problems was that Sonny liked to work too much—and I didn't."

WHEN SHE KNEW THE MARRIAGE WAS DISINTEGRATING: At 4:30 a.m. Oct. 27, 1972 — she just woke up and told Sonny she was splitting for San Francisco and asked him for $300. He calmly agreed.

FANTASY PLAYTHING: Elvis Presley

can still see the mobs of people on the highway leaving Da Nang, crushed into the boats, and trying to jam themselves inside helicopters and planes that were already full.

"When the news came that Da Nang would soon fall to the NVA, I put my things on my bicycle and took the highway south, out of the city. But so many people were doing the same thing, the road became jammed."

Lien turned around and bicycled to the shore. The American ships anchored off the coast

continued page 123

PINK
PROFILE

Randall Floyd

Nickname: Pink.

Survival skills: Low key, affable and flexible as a result of his family moving every year or so, he straddles various cliques with ease.

Critical influences: His father, the Green Bay Packers, and the Vietnam War. His father regaled his son with stories of wacko brass and incomprehensible bureaucracy. Bart Starr's brilliant, unpretentious quarterbacking for the Packers offered a blueprint for cool behavior. Pink supported the Vietnam War mainly because he identified it with his father's patriotism. Both of them changed their minds about the same time. His dad left the Army; Pink grew his hair long.

Theme song: "Careful With That Ax, Eugene" by his namesakes.

Literary hero: Kurt Vonnegut, Jr., author of <u>Slaughterhouse-Five</u> and <u>Mother Night</u>, though he's just read <u>A Fan's Notes</u>, Frederick Exley's 1968 novel about a football obsessive (and the great unsung cult paperback of the seventies). Pink thinks it may be the greatest book ever written.

Sports intrigue: Pittsburgh Pirates player Dock Ellis, who is rumored to have pitched a no-hitter while tripping on acid.

Talismans: A Les Paul guitar just like Jimmy Page's; his lucky pair of white Converse high-tops.

Least favorite warm up exercise: Squat thrusts. No one really looks cool doing them and saying it is sort of a drag too.

Fantasy product endorsement as jock/star: Owl memorabilia. Leave panty hose to Broadway Joe; owls do their best work at night, can turn their heads all the way around like Linda Blair and are just bad-ass birds of prey.

Unlikely cathode hero: Jack Lord as Steve McGarrett in Hawaii Five-O. The intro. with the war canoes and groovin' song rules as well as the native chicks in the sun with the pom pom skirts. Serious rays, the kickin' surf and puka shells for the asking. It's a real drag when Danno has to book a fairly righteous amount of pot though.

Ramblin' ambition: Hit the road after high school to see what the real world is like, inspired by the hero of Jack Kerouac's <u>On the Road</u> and repeated viewings of *The Last Detail*.

PLEDGE

Student Athlete Summer Pledge

May 26, 1976

I voluntarily agree to not indulge in any alcohol, drugs, or engage in any other illegal activity that may in any way jeopardize the years of hard work we as a team have committed to our goal of a championship season in '76'.

Signed_____

PROFILES in CONFUSION

New Sports Heroes

SPORTS SPECIAL FOR THE REBEL YELL

APRIL 21, 1976

AN EDITORIAL BY RANDALL FLOYD

"The New Role Model"

Quick, who do you think of when you hear the phrase, "perfect role model?" I will bet some of you thought of Roger Staubach, the scrambling quarterback of the Cowboys, or maybe a guy like Walter Cronkite.

Sorry folks, but my role models have never been the so-called "All-American" ones. Instead of clean-cut Tom Seaver, my baseball hero is Reggie Jackson — a guy who speaks his mind and is not afraid to show a little emotion. He makes baseball (a fairly boring sport to me) that much more exciting when he is on the field. Give me the goatee and behind-the-back flair of Pistol Pete Maravich over the traditional John Havlicek. Why? Because these guys are not afraid to go against the grain, to take chances. After all, this is what our country seems to be so proud to boast — an independent mind. Unfortunately, this is more theory than what is actually practiced.

My all-time role model is Joe Willie Namath. This is an athlete who has revolutionized the sports world. He helped bring white shoes, long hair, and style to a game long considered Neanderthal. Many people dislike his cockiness and would look more to someone like Johnny Unitas as a better role model. Unitas may have better statistics and a flat-top, but Namath has boosted pro football's popularity and has led the way for players to start thinking for themselves. It was Namath, with his long hair and white cleats that led the Jets to an upset

victory over the Johnny Unitas-style Colts in the 1969 Superbowl. Broadway Joe changed the "face" of sports forever. You don't have to look like Wally Cleaver to be a great athlete.

Let's face it, being clean-cut doesn't mean much anymore. The outrageous book Ball Four showed that baseball players are definitely not angels. Baseball, booze and sex is more accurate than baseball, hot dogs and apple pie. Take Babe Ruth for instance. Despite hitting 714 home runs and being loved by thousands of kids, Babe Ruth was seen chasing girls and was a regular at most of New York City's night clubs. This is the point: he did it on the playing field and that is what counts. This country has to quit worrying about how things look, whether the image is right, and think more about the results.

87

WOODERSON *PROFILE*

DAVID WOODERSON

EARLY ROLE MODEL:
Steve McQueen in Bullet.

YOUTHFUL PURSUITS:
Drag racing, mummifying yards with toilet paper, rocking all night long to Stones, Who, Doobies, Black Sabbath, Little Feat, Black Oak Arkansas, Marshall Tucker and others, playing poker, cruising for chicks, getting mellow, shooting pool.

MENTOR: His uncle Jimmy "Angles" Beausoleil, a low level racketeer from New Orleans who tells him, "Kid, people basically got freedom when dey come into dis oith, but all over da woild you see 'em woikin nine to five so dey can watch TV with da ball and chain. Even bein' rich don't get you outta bein' in a pine box someday. So I say eat good, get lotsa nookie, and don't sweat da small stuff."

GROWN-UP PURSUITS:
Following graduation (Class of '74), gets job operating photo machine for driver's license bureau; otherwise same as above.

HERO: Joe Don Looney, the great "what-me-worry?" running back for the Detroit Lions.

LIFESTYLE ACCESSORIES: Apartment in singles complex, Dura-Float lap-seam waterbed, quadraphonic stereo and three or four quad LPs, day-glo stars on ceiling over bed, wall-to-wall shag carpeting, zodiac poster featuring sexual positions, five years of Playboy, cannabis refrigerator magnets.

FAVORITE BELT BUCKLE: Messiah pot leaf: a waving Jesus in soft green hue with dope smoke halo.

MANUAL SKILL: While driving, can roll perfect joints one-handed when steering with his knees.

THEME SONG:
"I Just Wanna Make Love to You" by Foghat.

NOTABLE QUOTABLES:
"Alright, alright, alright. Gotta joint? It'd be a lot cooler if you did."

AMBITION:
Fulfill Bob Dylan's imperative to "Keep on Keepin' On."

Gun-Toting Dames Are A Bummer And Must Be Stopped

by Kevin Pickford

The other night, my girlfriend heard The Captain and Tenille on the radio. "I think it's so cool that they're so happy and look so good on TV," she says. "I mean, I not only like what they're singing about, but how they made it to the top together, fifty-fifty, and are so-ooh in love."

I told her I thought it was cool that girls are making attempts to progress in society, including rock 'n' roll. Personally, I support the Equal Rights Amendment, and when I get married, I'll have no problems with my old lady working until she settles down and decides to have kids. But man, there's some really bad vibes in this Women's Lib "fifty-fifty" thing, and I don't mean burning their bras. In some areas, they've tried to get too far too soon and started freak-ing out. Take ter-rorist acts for example. Man, something has to be done about these chicks who are toting guns. I mean, come on, what's their deal?

In September 1975, they were out of control. First, there's Lynette "Squeaky" Fromme, some Charles Manson squeeze who wanted to kill President Ford. Well, actually, there were, like, four bullets in Fromme's gun, but she said she didn't shoot on purpose because all she really wanted to do was to draw attention to concerns about the environment.

Right on, Squeaky. Save the planet, kill a guy. A real hero for Mother Earth, she told police how she and her roommate Sandra Good only had a little bread and salvaged things out of garbage cans to live off of, but that the quality of stuff people threw out had gone way down. What a chick!

Then there's Patty Hearst — oh, I'm sorry, is she calling herself "Tania" these days? Poor little rich girl, or poor little "self-employed urban guerrilla," as she signed the jail house register. OK, man, I'm like real bummed that she got kidnapped and tortured by the Symbionese Liberation Army, but did that really cause her to cop out and take part in the bank robbery or fall in love with the group's leader Cinque (aka Donald DeFreeze), as well as SLA member William "Cujo" Wolfe?

Finally there's Sara Jane Moore, a relatively normal 45-year-old divorced mom from the sub-urbs turned FBI snitch, leftist groupie, and would-be assassin, who, like Squeaky, wanted to snuff President Ford. Like, I'd heard that she had "grown to think of assassina-tion as a valid political tool when it was used selec-tively and with the purpose clearly and publicly stat-ed." Pretty far-out language lady — now why aren't you concentrating more on the PTA?

continued page 125

SABRINA
PROFILE

Sabrina Davis

Girlhood trauma:
Watched the regular fall broadcast of *The Wizard of Oz* alone one year because her mother was off working a catering gig. A terrible storm passes through in real life at the same time as in the movie, scaring Sabrina half to death and leading to a long period of intense identification with Dorothy Gale.

Likes: Horses, as reflected by the huge full-color poster of Secretariat on her wall, Bread's *Greatest Hits*, and Elton John, especially *Good-bye Yellow Brick Road*. Fought back tears the first time she heard "It seems you lived your life / like a candle in the wind."

Pet peeve: Her mother's E.S.T. rants which don't make any sense to her. Except for the saying "be here now" which seems obvious to her. Reminds her of the book she read last year, Free to Be You and Me by Marlo Thomas.

Dislikes: Most of her mother's boyfriends, especially when they try to charm her at breakfast, as if they weren't unshaven and in their underwear.

Slumber party adventure:
Successfully played the "I know who you are and I saw what you did" trick on Mr. Kaufman, a math teacher who kept making her do hard problems in front of the class.

Current crush:
John Travolta, who plays Vinnie Barbarino on TV's *Welcome Back, Kotter*.

Favorite book:
Watership Down, Richard Adams' bunny rabbit allegory. She thinks it would be even better if the rabbits were horses.

Favorite song: Neil Diamond's "Longfellow Serenade."

BURT REYNOLDS

NAME: Burt Reynolds

BIRTH DATE: February 11, 1936

BIRTH PLACE: Waycross, Georgia

HAIR: Brown

EYES: Brown

SIGN: Aquarius

HERITAGE: Italian-Cherokee

FIRST FILM: Angel Baby

RECENT FILMS: At Long Last Love, Lucky Lady, Hustle

CHILDHOOD: Grew up in Palm Beach, Florida where his dad was police chief; ran away from home at age 14 but later returned.

PAST LIVES: All-star football player at Florida State University; in New York, dishwasher at Scrafft's and bouncer at Roseland; stuntman; nude centerfold in Cosmopolitan magazine.

HOW HE GOT INTO SHOWBIZ: A football injury and car accident forced him to give up a sports career and choose college dramatics. Soon after, he quit college and moved to New York in 1955, where he eventually got a part in a revival of "Mr. Roberts." This led to a contract with Universal.

ROLE HE TURNED DOWN: TV series M*A*S*H

PAST PLAYTHING: Judy "Sock It To Me" Carne

PRESENT PLAYTHING: Dinah Shore, 19 years his senior

RECENT ANNIVERSARY PRESENTS: He to her— a TV tape machine; she to him— a pool table and sauna in her home for his use.

POSSIBLE SIGN OF STRAYING: He's recently been seen with Lorna Luft, Liza Minelli's half sister.

MICHELLE'S BETTER CROCKED BROWNIES

All of you have been asking me, *"How do you make those bitchin brownies?"* Well, to tell you the truth, I found the recipe in my mom's closet, next to her leftover Hooka from her hippie days. But since going out with **Pickford,** and experimenting with the different kinds of pot he's been selling, I've customized the recipe, making the preparation time a little more bearable. During one part of the recipe, there's a lot of time to kill. I killed it by painting **Gene** and **Ace** on the statues of our Founding Fathers that Benny and Pink stole from the Savings and Loan.

WARNING: This recipe requires a bit of menial labor so it is recommended that preceding this culinary experience you inhale some large bong hits.

INGREDIENTS:
2 boxes of your favorite brownie mix—and all the ingredients. You are going to follow the recipe on the back of the brownie box but there will be one small addition. When it calls for the oil you will use the pot butter instead. If the recipe calls for 1/3 cup of oil, use 1/3 cup of butter or margarine plus the pot.
1 quarter of mid-grade pot. (If you've just bought some sensemilia, don't bother baking, just load up a big bowl.)
ACCESSORIES:
1 Frisbee or album cover
1 Student ID. card or a matchbook will do
1 Coffee bean grinder, or hammer it into a pulp with something, you know, like a hammer and some paper towels.

When choosing your brownie mix make sure that the recipe calls for oil; I don't recommend getting the kind with frosting because these brownies are really rich and frosting will make you want to puke.

At some point *the pot needs to be cleaned.* This is when the bong hit comes in. This can be a very pleasurable and rewarding experience if accompanied by your favorite TV. show, like an episode of **Beverly Hillbillies**. Use your ID. card and the Frisbee to clean the pot. Remove all of the stems and seeds you can. This takes the "woody" taste out of the brownies.

Throw the pot into a **coffee grinder** so it comes out in a powdered form. After you have powdered the pot, add the butter; put it in a pan to slowly simmer. This process will take about 3 hours. The best time to do this part is on a Saturday morning around ten. This way there is about an hour of **cartoons** and then a **Japanese monster movie** comes on. This task does take a little skill because the butter cannot be allowed to burn, so I recommend putting it on the lowest setting and stirring every ten minutes or so. When **Godzilla** dies you know your butter is ready. Now just follow the recipe that's on the back of the box.

Another hint is to make sure that there are alternate munchies around because when your brownies kick in you don't want to forage on too many of them.

Pot Etiquette

HELPFUL HINTS FROM WOODERSON

- When rolling a joint, do not lick the whole joint for a "slow burn."

- Hogging the reefer to yourself is often known as "Bogarting," punishable by death.

- Never roll your weed with "lumber" (sticks/stems).

- Always roll with one paper.

- Never roll a "pop-corn joint" (marijuana cigarettes with seeds).

- Always de-seed and de-stem your pot.

- Never criticize another's weed after smoking it.

- Always hold in smoke for 2.3 minutes, then cough a lot through nose in appreciation.

- After smoking, play "Physical Graffiti" as loud as possible.

- Don't mooch pot off others, unless others mooch pot off you.

- Never spill the Bong water.

- Don't ever drink the Bong water (even if it's a beer bong).

- Never talk when holding the joint (unless in Europe).

- Don't scrape your friend's pipes.

- Don't skim others bags.

- Always sell full, five finger bags.

- Save roaches for a rainy day (or dry periods).

- Don't hand someone a clogged bong.

- Never pass a microscopic roach.

- Don't light cigarettes off the joint.

- Don't light joints off the cigarette.

-*Never ever narc.*

Don Dawson
3rd Period English
Book Report
April 16, 1976

At last a book that speaks to me: How to Pick Up Girls. Twenty-five cuties give all the inside dope on how to score with them. The hard vs. the soft approach, what to say to a college girl at the produce section, alcohol and the opening line, first impressions and falling down, they're all here. Each chapter a treasure, in each sentence a gem. For the nerd who has loved and lost a lot, How to Pick Up Girls is a babe-bagging manifesto.

A secretary reveals some pointers on being chatted up at the laundromat and in the lobby of a movie theater. Another subject is tackled by two sophomores from Vassar. "How to get her attention when she's reading by the pool." An unnamed professional tennis player is turned on by the man who 'makes a pass at her while she is dining.' (Perhaps she associates food with sex?!) In one experience she describes a love note she received from the waiter in a hollowed out buttered scone. By last call he might as well have been in nothing but silk pajamas and a pipe by a pinball machine.

It isn't strictly a self help type book. If a guy really and truly cannot score in one form or another, somewhere with someone even with blinding dumb luck, perhaps professional help is in order. I always suggest medical attention to the dude that didn't get his candle waxed come Monday. I personally don't need to be told what gets a girl horny; finding out is half the fun.

How to Pick Up Girls gets into the single's bar scene which is kind of hard to apply to the average high school goof. Also, everyone's Fred Astaire after loosening up with a few drinks, (Chapter 42: Putting on the Moves on the Dance Floor). I'll trade a well pronounced chin and sexy smile for "a sense of humor and an inner sense of self awareness" any day of the week, (Chapter 71: The Boy Inside the Man). Though I disagree in a few instances and the book doesn't shed any new light personally I highly recommend How to Pick Up Girls. It's perfect for the dashboard, the locker room, and the bathroom. The list of the fifty great opening lines should be showing up on refrigerators across this great country soon.

CLINT PROFILE

Clint Bruno

EARLY ENVIRONMENT: Clint's dad usually entered the house like he was sorry he forgot to smash the door into splinters, which created plenty of tension and drove the kids into petty crime, moto-cross racing, and promiscuity.

COVETED TROPHY: Quarter midget state champion, 1970.

EARLY ESCAPIST FARE: All the violent TV stuff, like *The Rifleman, The Rebel, Combat, Branded, Hawk, Hawaii Five-O, N.Y.P.D.*, and *Mannix*.

BOYHOOD FANTASY: Joining the Rat Pack, (not Frank Sinatra's clique but) the World War II guys on TV who rode around in jeeps with rear-mounted machine guns and flushed most of the Germans out of North Africa.

FLIRTING TECHNIQUES: Bra snapping, growling, piston-and-cylinder hand gesture (and the odd knowing glance up a dress).

SECRET CRUSH: Susan Dey, who plays Laurie on TV.'s *The Partridge Family*.

FRESHMAN HARASSMENT TRICK: Open-handed book dump in the hallways between classes, often followed by a foot-trip when the kid goes after his scattered textbooks.

MUSICAL INSPIRATION: Ted Nugent's *Call of the Wild*.

FAVORITE GAME PIECE: Always gets the car during smoke-out strip Monopoly™ sessions.

TATTOOS: Left arm, Phoenix (vulture on fire). Right arm: "Mama Tried," in bold Roman lettering.

LIFE AFFIRMING QUOTE: "If you want a tattoo cheap, you're gonna get a cheap tattoo."

FAVORITE MUSCLE T-SHIRT: A white one for day work; a black one for night maneuvers.

PRIZED POSSESSION: New white '76 Trans Am. Paid cash for it after working at his neighbor's gas station four years straight.

HOW TO PICK UP GIRLS!
by Eric Weber

Featuring interviews
with 25 beautiful girls!

Straight

The following is a transcript of a White House press conference given by President Ford on March 1, 1975, for no particular reason.

Talk

Straight Talk reprinted from *National Lampoon*

Members of the Press, networks, commentators, foreign correspondents, opinion-makers, White House watchers, writers for posterity, and so on — let me punt off by saying a very warm good morning to the both of you. As you know, I am prone to crack some little jokes before getting down to the business of making a fool of myself, and I frankly see no reason why this should be an exception where this excellent method of staving off the sweat-treatment is concerned. Unfortunately, my comedy consultant, Mr. William Buckley, was unable to come up with anything much except GOP elephant jokes and a bunch of lame puns about shooting Feisal out of a barrel, but Nelson told me a real knee-slapper. How do you know when the CIA has been in your fridge? Any hands? Okay, answer: You don't. Thank you. Okay, yes you, over there, sitting next to the Weatherman?

Q. Sir, there are indications that whatever is being done, the depression is deepening. Nonetheless, your administration keeps denying there is one. Could you explain this?

A. I want to be quite frank with you about this question of the depression and my handling of it. There are no two ways about it — I am bad and I'm going to get worse. Much, much worse. One of the good things about a depression, however, is that the last thing people want to hear about is politics. It only makes them more depressed. So I figure the worse I can make this depression the less people are going to be able to face checking up on me. They'll just pop off to *The Towering Inferno* or jump off a ledge and forget the whole thing. And that, I think, is the right way to react. In these terrible times, the best thing all Americans can do is to take life less seriously.

Well Kept Celebrity Secrets

Euell Gibbons

Evel Knievel

Except the CIA, of course. They can take life any way they want and wherever they deem fit.

Q. Mr. President, do you have any reaction to the mounting evidence that the CIA conducted illegal domestic counterintelligence operations during the sixties and early seventies?

A. Well, I suppose the easy way out here would be to tell the truth, and say quite candidly that I have no reaction to that whatsoever. (I find this to be the case with many such reports I receive and, believe me, you sleep a lot easier.) However, since I can see that you're not going to let this one go, perhaps this reaction of mine Ron just handed to me might clear it up for all of us. It says here this is a three-fold problem. First there's the domestic problem. Rocky tells me, for example, that he's been seeking a bootblack for his chauffeur's butler all winter. Actually, I must have meant that as a joke and this CIA thing is really only a two-fold problem.

Secondly, the operations themselves. I think I can safely say that anything the CIA did definitely ran counter to intelligence. The agency, during the time in question, discovered a lot of intelligent people thinking intelligent things - things that ran counter to national security as well. This had to be stopped. So they simply used counterintelligence, or if you prefer, stupidity, to bring this nation through those desperate times into these.

And it worked. We all know that there's nothing too intelligent about an effete snob of the Kennedy mold - say, like yourself sir — if he's looking down the business end of a silencer that makes a 30.06 hunting rifle sound like a squirrel fart.

Thirdly, as for the illegality of it, I cannot judge. This is a matter for the Supreme Court to rule on just as soon as Douglas croaks and I can stuff someone in there who'll make Burger look like a Berrigan brother. Yes, you, over there?

Q. Could you explain, sir, why the appointees to the blue-ribbon CIA investigatory panel were almost all members of the defense establishment?

A. Now, that's an easy one. As you should know from your high school civics book, Don, everything a good CIA does is secret. We can't let just anybody go thrashing through all the microfilm; otherwise they wouldn't be secrets anymore, if you follow. By appointing only folks who already know the secrets, we can restore public confidence in the CIA's other secrets — you know, the scary ones.

Q. But surely, sir, the purpose of the panel was to eradicate the atmosphere of secrecy?

A. Well, if it was, I haven't been told. Of course, that might be a secret, too — I'm not that hot on keeping them myself, as, for example, my deal with Dick. After all, America can't squander its limited reserves of secrets — particularly when the Soviets have so many more than the United States. Mr. Breshnog himself, for instance, has leukemia. Now why can't the President have secrets like that? Heck, I don't even know if Betty has two months or two years and I run all the H-bombs. In theory, anyway. Over in the back. Yes?

Q. Mr. President, Secretary Kissinger recently repeated that the United States might take military action against Middle East oil-producers if their policies resulted in a strangulation of industrialized nations. Can you tell us if you agree and under what conditions this might occur?

A. Well, let me say, in answer to the first part of your highly embarrassing question, that when it comes to date-munchers, you don't disagree with Hank. As I was saying just this morning to whoever's in charge of the economy this week: You know how to make a Nazi cross? Kick him in the policies, that's how. Then again, if Nancy's on the rag, Hank starts blaming the whole world — like when he purposely pissed on the Shah of Iran's best carpet because Nancy had a sore fetlock.

Secondly, when it comes to broiling Arabs, I must repeat that under my policy of decentralization, I feel the State Department should take full responsibility for more of these split-second decisions and inform me if, and only if, one of those decisions is headed for Washington so I'll have time to sprint for the helicopter.

And fourthly, I have nothing further to say about those other two or three points.

Q. But sir, certainly you can't just turn a blind eye to a decision as sensitive an invading the Middle East?

A. Oh? Well, you better take another think, pal. All I, or anyone, knows is if the Dow

continued page 124

Barbra Streisand

NAME: Barbra Streisand

BIRTH DATE: April 24, 1942

BIRTH PLACE: Brooklyn, New York

HAIR: Blonde

EYES: Blue

SIGN: Taurus

FIRST ACTING BREAK: In 1962 in "I Can Get It For You Wholesale" in which she played Yetta Tessye Marmelstein and won the New York Critics Award.

FILM CREDITS: *Funny Girl, Hello Dolly!, On A Clear Day You Can See Forever, The Owl and the Pussycat, What's Up Doc, Up the Sandbox, The Way We Were, For Pete's Sake, Funny Lady, A Star Is Born*

ACHIEVEMENTS: Won Oscar for her role in *Funny Girl*

FEELINGS ABOUT FAME: "To me the whole idea of being a star is a pain."

PAST PLAYTHINGS: ex-hubby Elliott Gould (who she met in "I Can Get It For You Wholesale"), Ryan O'Neal, Burt Bacharach, Pierre Trudeau, Sam Grossman (allegedly)

MOST RECENT PLAYTHING: Hair dresser Jon Peters, ex-hubby of Leslie Ann Warren: "He's treating me like a woman. Not some famous thing."

WHO SHE'D LIKE TO WORK WITH: Elvis Presley

Fred O'Bannion
3rd Period English
Book Report

Mrs. Clinkingbeard, I have decided not to do the book report assignment on "The Old Man and the Sea." An old guy and a boy and a boat and a big fish and some sea; very boring. Had his name been Quint and it was one big shark I'm sure the tale would have been scarier and thus more interesting. Also, if he is such a Christ figure as the Cliff Notes indicate, why doesn't he just pick up "Moby" and drag him back to shore on foot?

Rather than doing another hum drum essay let's turn our attention to a more pressing matter that I'm sure you and the other teachers have pondered during your butt breaks in the lounge. What if Huggy Bear (from "Starsky and Hutch") and Rooster (from "Baretta") got into a major pimp fight... Who would win?

Huggy bear is shrewd and has some good disguises but Rooster probably has the reach. Huggy Bear has a cool car but Rooster has the bitches and dynamite feathers. Actually whether or not "Starsky" has a plush ride has little bearing on the outcome of the pimp rumble. Billy is Baretta's friend and father figure. He taught Fred (a wily cockatoo) to answer the phone, drink cheap wine and curse. I have seen Billy in a movie with Marilyn Monroe so I know he is pretty together for an old fart. Rooster mumbles and complains a lot but his hats are huge!! Huggy Bear vs. Rooster and Baretta and Hutch — his guitar x Fred and Billy drunk = Coolsville!

Watching at the end of the rat flanked alley stands the smoky silhouette of Rooster. Huggy is holding court by the fire exit of his place; Huggy's place. A doobie is being passed among some of the closing patrons, a few select lucky bitches and Sammy Davis Jr. Rooster approaches giving his purple boa a confident toss over his left shoulder.

"Don't do the dime if you can't do the time!" says Rooster tauntingly. He takes a long slow drag on his cigarette holder and blows a perfect menthol hoop of smoke around Sammy's "Have a nice day" face medallion. No one is amused.

"Funny... I don't remember orderin' no pizza?" Huggy Bear chortles. In one great bristling of plumes and hounds tooth topcoats, the crowd scatters to various pockets of the alley. Huggy Bear squares off throwing his denim boogie hat against a crumpled trash can. With a quick turn of his ivory horse-head walking cane he brandishes a hidden sword. Rooster's eyes widen and whiten looking like freshly twisted oreos.

"Peace my brothers!" Sammy chirps, "We got to fight the man not among ourselves!"

Sammy pleads in vain to stop the scuffle but it is too late. With the precision of a martial artist or maybe a surgeon, he kabobs Rooster like a Spanish olive with a swizzle stick. Sammy swoons and is carried off by the rhythm section of the Ohio Players, murmuring something about "Da judge coming," and "Keeping your eye on the Pharaoh."

"Dats da name of dat tune," adds Huggy triumphantly. He pulls out his fist handled fro pick and pulls at his sculpted coif. Just another day in the life of a man of the street. He twists Rooster's cigarette into the ground with the heel of his seven inch acrylic platforms. It is obvious to everybody who is the baddest struttin' mofo on the scene.

I hope this has been a breath of fresh air. I believe you'll feel the same way once you have plodded through a dozen or so plot summaries of "The Old Man and the Sea."

Bruno's Pot

BRUNO'S "SECRET SLANG" FOR THE SMOKING OF MARIJUANA
(Great for using on 'hot' phones or the listening uninitiated)

- One way ticket to Sugartown
- Heading out
- Sparked up
- Thumpin' buggers out the window

WHO'S REALLY IN CONTROL?

THE REBEL YELL
MAY, 1976
BY CYNTHIA DUNN

The eagerly-awaited movie version of how Watergate became public knowledge through the investigative efforts of two reporters from **The Washington Post** — **ALL THE PRESIDENT'S MEN** (starring Robert Redford as Bob Woodward and Dustin Hoffman as Carl Bernstein) has finally arrived. And, I'm somewhat disappointed by the movie. The acting is good, the script is good, and the photography is good. So, what's wrong with it? Maybe it's just me, but I found the movie to be too long and anticlimactic, which made it dull. I thought that it would be able to stir the same excitement and suspense I felt when Watergate was actually occurring just a few years ago, but it didn't happen. Predictably, in the movie — as in real life — the goodness of truth overcomes the evils caused by the obstruction of justice perpetrated by the president, and our whole system of government returns to normal. Or, does it? If it was so easy for former President Nixon to run amok, committing crimes in what is supposed to be the highest, most sacred office in our nation, who's to say that the executive, legislative and judicial branches of our government are nothing more than fronts to hide a select chosen few who are <u>really</u> in control of this country? Perhaps our nation is being run by a secret society of sorts—like in **THE PARALLAX VIEW** — where "unacceptable" politicians and "questionable" private citizens are randomly killed when they come to close to discovering

WHO'S REALLY IN CONTROL?

Smoking Slang

- •Take a seat on the green couch
- •Blow a fatty
- •Twisting
- •Dressed up for the ball

- •Holdin' court with Kris Greengle
- •Spanking handsome Jim
- •Cut the cake
- •Who farted
- •Spacing in

- •Touching the face of Godot
- •Tickling the ivories
- •Slappin' Jackyls
- •The boss gets fired (The boss is getting fired)

Warren Beatty

NAME: Warren Beatty

BIRTH DATE: March 30, 1937

BIRTH PLACE: Richmond, Virginia

HAIR: Brown

EYES: Blue

SIGN: Aries

PAST LIFE: A construction worker

WHAT HE COULD HAVE BEEN: A football player— he turned down 10 college scholarships.

FIRST FILM: *Splendor in the Grass*

RECENT FILMS: *Shampoo, The Fortune*

HOW HE BROKE INTO SHOWBIZ: With his older sister Shirley MacLaine, he started acting as a child in amateur productions directed by his mother, a drama coach.

PAST POLITICS: George McGovern in 1972

ROLES HE'S TURNED DOWN BECAUSE HE'S SO BORED WITH HIS OWN STARDOM: *The Sting, Butch Cassidy and the Sundance Kid, Last Tango in Paris, The Great Gatsby*

ROLE HE WANTS: To play Howard Hughes

HIS RECENT PENTHOUSE AT THE BEVERLY WILSHIRE: As disheveled as his hair

HIS NEW MERCEDES: As disheveled as his penthouse

PAST PLAYTHINGS: Joan Collins, Natalie Wood, Leslie Caron, Julie Christie, Carly Simon (who wrote "You're So Vain" in his honor), Joni Mitchell, Liv Ullman, and most recently, Michelle Phillips.

by David Wooderson

You may laugh at the words foosball and Zen appearing in the same sentence, but for some people it only takes one time behind the bars, watching as your team moves back and forth, performing some crazy dance that you have choreographed. As you stare down at the shiny helmets of your opponent the ball spins wildly around the table — sometimes so fast you can't even see it fly. You react with that "sixth sense", you become one with the table and you're hooked. And when I say hooked, I mean as dedicated to that game as any religious fanatic could be devoted to a god. Driven like a Muslim to Mecca your pilgrimage is to the parlor. Pure passion pulls you through that door as you search for partners and opponents to convert. You feel the spirit as surely as you feel the handles in your palms. The river flows in one direction and that's toward the goal as you search for salvation in the form of that unmistakable sound. It's something like a cross between a wooden bat cracking a home run and a large coin falling in a slot machine. Score!

Last night was probably one of my most inspirational evenings. Whoever was in charge of the jukebox must have been a genius — Aerosmith cranking us up and Pink Floyd mellowing us out. The first team my partner Kyle and I played was George and Esther. Esther had some wicked angles.

An angle shot is a little different from the type of shot people usually make during a game. It involves shooting the ball diagonally. Most people prefer to push, pull, or set-up the ball so they can hit it straight on and force it into the hole. An angle shot, however, takes a lot of finesse and technique to be able to get it to go in a diagonal line accurately enough to be effective. When you make an angle shot from the front lines there are some areas that simply cannot be blocked — if you're accurate enough.

Fortunately Kyle had a great serve. It's against the rules for you to put your finger all the way through the hole when you're serving on to the table because, if you stick your finger all the way through the hole, you can push it from one side to the other and give the ball to your own man. So to circumvent that, Tim had learned how to put a back spin on the ball and make it pop out on to the table, spin for a moment, and then, as it slowed down, roll towards his man every time. That way he could pass the ball to his forward man where he could make a shot at the goal.

I think at this point we ought to talk a little about middle-men or five-man shots. In Texas they don't allow you to serve the ball and then immediately shoot or grab hold of it and shoot from the middle men (the first row of five men at the center of the table). Apparently in the Midwest, they allow you to do that. I personally don't have a problem with this if you're playing a team, especially because it just means that there's an extra set of men guarding the goal. If you are playing singles, however, I could see how it could be a little unfair to because you don't have any way of moving the row of

ZEN AND THE ART OF PLAYING FOOSBALL

men in the back defending their goal. But hey, "When in Rome, do as the Romans do."

There are nine balls on the table and you can't bring any of them back. Unless, of course, you hit it hard enough that it goes in one goal, bounces through the tray in the bottom of the table, and comes back out the other side — something that I've seen happen quite a few times on both Tornado and Dynamo tables.

One of my best shots is just a regular pull. A pull shot involves getting your man in front of the ball and shooting it straight towards the goal. You pull the ball towards yourself, let it go, then speed past it, and when it's in front of your man again, flick your wrist, and then it's speeding towards the goal. It's all in the pull and flick. Well, my pull shot is pretty darn fast, if I say so myself. Another type of shot is called a push shot which is a mirror image of the pull shot.

My other hot shot is a set-up. You have three men at the front of the table that you can shoot from: one in the middle and a man on either side. To do a set-up, you pass the ball to the man in the middle from one of the men on the sides. When I do my set-ups, I usually bat it back and forth more than a couple of times, waiting for my opponent to either move out of the way or be so confused that he stands still for a second and creates a hole for me to shoot through.

My partner had a rockin' bank shot. A bank shot is usually from the back, but Tim was so good he could do it from the front. A bank shot involves banking the ball off the side of the table on it's way toward the goal at the other end of the table. It's super-effective because foosball men aren't set up for angles. They're set up for straight shots. You just can't compensate for some of the space between the bars. If your accurate with this shot, it can be deadly.

This is a good time to interject a little bit about the differences in foosball tables. There's really only two foosball table manufacturers: Dynamo and Tornado. If you're a multiple bank shot player or if you really, really like speed, Tornado is the way to go. They have a slicker table and their balls are much harder and they never get gummy. The Dynamo surface is somewhat corrugated, so the balls get a little gummier. When the balls do get gummy some people call them "gumballs" (not to be confused with the meatball which is the last ball of the game.) Some people hate gumballs, but some prefer the extra traction. The good thing about a gumball is it's great for making toe shots. At one time or another a player will have their man resting on the ball — either in front or behind the ball. You can catch the ball like that or you may set it up that way on purpose to make a toe shot. The good thing about a toe shot is you can move the ball in either direction to the right or the left of your opponent and shoot.

But all this technical jargon is a little distracting. Where's the Zen? Where's the river flowing? Where's that "sound" I talked about? It's the sound that makes you high when you're on the offense. It's the cloud you ride when you become one with the table. Tonight, that sound was all around us. It seemed like we could do no wrong. A dollar and a half — at the most — and we stayed on the table all night. Exhausted, we finally gave up, went outside, smoked a little pot, and decided to spend the rest of the evening in the park. We'll be back.

The foosball parlor: it opens at five. My friends and I will all be there at four-thirty out in the parking lot waiting for the owner to open the place up, and the ritual will begin all over again.

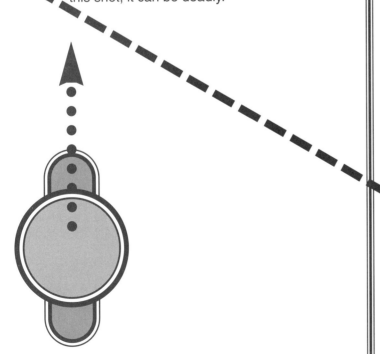

A Dazed & Confused

TIMELINE

September 1973: The class of '77 begins their freshman year of High School.

Sept. 1, 1973: Last episode of *H.R. Pufnstuf* airs on ABC-TV. The show had followed Jimmy and his talking flute, Freddie, stuck on an island occupied by Mayor H.R. Pufnstuf, along with the evil Witchiepoo who constantly tries to foil their attempts at escape, while trying to steal Freddie.

Sept. 2, 1973: J.R.R. Tolkien dies. His books include "The Hobbit" and "Lord of the Rings."

Sept. 6, 1973: At Watergate hearings, Pat Buchanan admits to an unethical 1972 Republican campaign.

Sept. 11, 1973: Military junta allegedly backed by the CIA overthrows Marxist government of Salvador Allende of Chile.

Sept. 19, 1973: Graham Parsons of the Flying Burrito Brothers dies from a multiple drug overdose while rehearsing in the desert outside Los Angeles.

Sept. 20, 1973: Jim Croce dies in plane crash en route to a performance at Austin College in Sherman Texas, two months after the release of his album "Time in a Bottle".

Sept. 20, 1973: Presenting him with a live "male chauvinist" pig, Billie Jean King defeats Bobby Riggs in "Battle of Sexes" tennis match.

Sept. 29, 1973: The DeFranco Family's "Heartbeat—It's a Lovebeat" hits #3 on *Billboard's* Top 40. Also on charts is Bob Dylan's "Knockin' On Heaven's Door" (#12), The Rolling Stones' "Angie" (#2), and Grand Funk Railroad's "We're an American Band" (#1).

Oct. 5, 1973: Oregon becomes the first state to decriminalize marijuana.

Oct. 9, 1973: Elvis and Priscilla Presley divorce.

Oct. 10, 1973: Spiro T. Agnew resigns as vice president on account of tax evasion.

Oct. 12, 1973: President Nixon announces Gerald R. Ford as Vice President.

1973

by Pamela Bruce and R.U. Stienberg

freshman year

Oct. 15, 1973: *The Tomorrow Show* premieres on late night NBC-TV with host Tom Snyder in a talk show format featuring unusual and controversial topics.

Oct. 17, 1973: Arab nations impose oil embargo on United States for its support of Israel during Oct. 6th Yom Kippur War.

Oct. 19, 1973: At Watergate hearings, John Dean pleads guilty to his role in cover-up.

Oct. 20, 1973: *The Six Million Dollar Man* premieres on ABC-TV. The show depicts the life of astronaut Steve Austin (played by Lee Majors) who has undergone a special life-saving bionic and cybernetic operation following a mishap during a test flight. Following the $6 million surgery he becomes an agent of the O.S.I (Office of Scientific Intelligence).

Oct. 20, 1973: President Nixon fires White House special prosecutor Archibald Cox, which results in resignations of Attorney General Richardson and his assistant William Ruckelhaus.

Oct. 23, 1973: Congress considers impeachment proceedings against President Nixon, who responds by releasing White House tapes to Judge John Sirica.

Nov. 17, 1973: President Nixon says, "I am not a crook."

December 1973: The movie *The Exorcist* is released. Adapted from the novel by William Peter Blatty, features the daughter of a Washington DC's highbrow family, possessed by Satan.

Dec. 1, 1973: The Carpenters' "Top of the World" hits #1 on *Billboard's* Top 40.

Dec. 8, 1973: Brownsville Station's "Smokin' in the Boy's Room" hits *Billboard's* Top 40.

Dec. 13, 1973: "Brain Salad Surgery" by Emerson, Lake, and Palmer goes gold.

Dec. 20, 1973: Bobby "Mack the Knife" Darin dies of heart failure.

Dec. 25, 1973: *The Sting* is released, featuring the team of Robert Redford and Paul Newman as con men.

Dec. 28, 1973: Comet Kohutek makes lackluster appearance. Discovered by Czechoslovakian astronomer Lubos Kohutek on March 7, 1973, the comet was a flop to most people, but pleased scientists on Earth and astronauts aboard Skylab 3.

1974

January 1974: *Last Tango in Paris* is released.

Jan. 2, 1974: President Nixon signs into law a bill requiring states to limit speed limits to 55 mph to receive federal highway trust funds.

Jan. 4, 1974: President Nixon rejects subpoena by Senate to release more than 500 tapes.

Jan. 11, 1974: Last episode of *Love American Style*, a show which depicts funny romantic entanglements, airs. It features a skit about two political opponents, James Hampton and Anne Randall, who fall in love; Arlene Golonka has a phobia about Larry Kent's apartment; Robert Morse and Elaine Joyce reunite after 50

years; there is a battle of the sexes between Bobby Riggs and Rosemary Casals; and finally, Larry Storch cannot sleep without a special clock, but Joyce Van Patten comes to the rescue.

Jan. 15, 1974: *Happy Days* premieres on ABC-TV. This nostalgic comedy about raising a family in the Eisenhower era stars Tom Bosley as father Howard Cunningham, Marion Ross as mother Marion, and Ron Howard as their son Richie. The show also features Anson Williams as Potsie Webber, Donny Most as Ralph Malph, and Henry Winkler as Arthur "Fonzie" Fonzirelli.

February 1974: *Blazing Saddles* is released, a western comedy by Mel Brooks, former writer for the Smothers Brothers.

Feb. 1, 1974: The first episode of the sit-com *Good Times* airs, starring Jimmy "J. J." Walker, as the son of a low income family living in the ghetto.

Feb. 2, 1974: "The Way We Were" by Barbra Streisand peaks at #1 on *Billboard's* Top 40.

Feb. 5, 1974: Patricia Hearst, daughter of newspaper mogul Randolph Hearst, is kidnapped in Berkeley, California by the Symbionese Liberation Army. They say they will release her if a multi-million dollar food program is institut-

ed for the poor. In reaction to their demands to feed the poor, California's governor Ronald Reagan later says, "It's too bad we can't have an epidemic of botulism."

Feb. 6, 1974: US House votes to begin impeachment proceedings against President Nixon.

Feb. 8, 1974: Skylab 3 astronauts return to Earth after record 84 day space flight.

Feb. 13, 1974: Russian author Alexsandr Solzhenitsyn, known for his book "The Gulag Archipelago," is deported by U.S.S.R. to West Germany.

Feb. 15, 1974: David Bowie releases "Rebel Rebel/Queen Bitch" single.

Feb. 15, 1974: Odd-even system for purchasing gasoline is adopted in seven states and Washington DC to cope with fuel shortages.

Feb. 19, 1974: KISS makes its debut TV appearance on Don Kirschner's *In Concert*.

Feb. 20, 1974: Cher files for separation from Sonny Bono after 10 years of marriage.

Feb. 29, 1974: Federal grand jury indicts eight former Ohio National Guard members on charges of violating the civil rights of four students who were shot to death and nine students who were injured during campus demonstration in May 1970 at Kent State University.

March 4, 1974: *People* magazine begins publication.

March 6, 1974: President Nixon says that he knew about Watergate hush money.

March 25, 1974: The Rolling Stones begin recording sessions for album "Black and Blue" at Musicland in Munich.

April 2, 1974: At the Academy Awards ceremony, Katherine Hepburn says, "I'm living proof someone can wait 41 years to be unselfish." *The Sting* wins seven. Tatum O'Neal becomes youngest recipient ever for her role in *Paper Moon*. Moments before David Niven announces Elizabeth Taylor's entrance, there's another Oscar night first — a streaker runs across stage. The streaker, later identified as 33-year-old Robert Opal, is found murdered five years later in San Francisco.

April 3, 1974: Internal Revenue Service declares that President Nixon owes $432,787 in back taxes and interest penalties totaling $33,000.

April 8, 1974: Hank Aaron breaks Babe Ruth's home run record by hitting his 715th.

April 11, 1974: House Judiciary Committee orders President Nixon to turn over tapes and other materials related to 42 White House conversations.

April 13, 1974: Elton John's "Bennie and the Jets" hits #1 on *Billboard's* Top 40.

April 24, 1974: Bud Abbott (of Abbott and Costello) dies.

April 25, 1974: Jim Morrison's widow Pamela dies from heroin overdose.

April 30, 1974: White House releases 1,200 pages of tape transcripts.

May 24, 1974: Duke Ellington dies.

May 24, 1974: *The Girl with Something Extra* is canceled after one short season leaving Sally Field and John Davidson with something less.

May 29, 1974: *Sonny and Cher Comedy Hour* airs last show. This repeat episode stars Joe Namath, the Righteous Brothers, and features regulars Bobby Hatfield, Teri Garr, Billy Van, Peter Cullen, and Freeman King.

June 1974: *Consumers' Research Magazine* announces "the new Polaroid SX-70 cam-

era," which is selling in the New York area for about $130.

June 1974: Roman Polanski's *Chinatown* is released.

June 11, 1974: Secretary of State Kissinger threatens to resign following charges that he conducted wire-taps.

June 27, 1974: *Flip Wilson Show* has its last telecast on NBC-TV. The former star of *Laugh-In*, Flip Wilson is known for his "Geraldine" and "Here Come the Judge" characters.

July 1974: Lucille Ball announces her retirement from weekly TV after 23 years.

July 1974: *High Times Magazine* debuts.

July 9, 1974: Crosby, Stills, Nash, and Young reunion tour begins.

July 24, 1974: US. Supreme Court rules that President Nixon must release all of his tapes.

July 27, 1974: House Judiciary Committee votes 27 to 11 to recommend to the House of Representatives that President Nixon be impeached.

July 29, 1974: Cass Elliot of the Mamas and Papas dies of a heart attack in London flat of

SUMMER '74
WATERGATE

'74 to '75

Harry Nilsson. False rumors spread that she dies choking on a ham sandwich.

Aug. 2, 1974: John Dean is sentenced to one-to-three years for his role in Watergate cover-up.

Aug. 5, 1974: Joan Jett forms an all-girl band, The Runaways.

Aug. 8, 1974: Richard Nixon announces his resignation as President of the United States.

Aug. 9, 1974: Gerald Ford becomes President of the United States.

Aug. 23, 1974: John Lennon reports seeing a UFO from the roof of his New York apartment at 9 p.m.

Aug. 30, 1974: Last episode of *The Brady Bunch* airs, a sitcom based on the marriage of a widow and widower, each with three siblings, three boys and three girls, airs on ABC-TV. This repeat episode, a pilot for a sequel series that never happened, features guest stars Ken Berry and Brooke Bundy as a childless couple who end up adopting three children.

Aug. 31, 1974: Last episode of *The Partridge Family* airs on ABC-TV.

Sept. 7, 1974: *Land of the Lost* premieres on NBC-TV's Saturday morning line-up. Exploring the Colorado River on a raft, forest ranger Rick Marshall and his children Will and Holly are caught in a time vortex that transports them to the mysterious, prehistoric Land of the Lost. Befriended by Chaka the monkey boy, the family searches for a way back home amid stampeding dinosaurs.

Sept. 8, 1974: Daredevil Evel Knievel fails to jump Snake Canyon on his specially equipped motorcycle/rocket.

Sept. 8, 1974: President Ford grants Richard Nixon a "full, free, and absolute pardon."

Sept. 9, 1974: A spin-off from *The Mary Tyler Moore Show*, (which features one of TV's first single working women, in an executive position), *Rhoda* premieres. The show depicts incidents in the life of Rhoda Morganstern (Valerie Harper), a window designer.

Sept. 11, 1974: *Little House on the Prairie* premieres on NBC-TV. Based on the "Little House" books by Laura Ingalls Wilder, the series is set in the town of Walnut Grove in Plumb Creek, Minnesota, during the 1870s

and follows the lives of the pioneering Ingalls family.

Sept. 13, 1974: *The Rockford Files* premieres on NBC-TV. The show depicts the exploits of Jim Rockford (played by James Garner), owner/operator of the Rockford Private Detective Agency, as he attempts to solve criminal cases that are considered unsolvable and labeled inactive by police.

Sept. 16, 1974: Bob Dylan begins recording sessions for the "Blood On The Tracks" LP.

Sept. 21, 1974: Jacqueline Susann, author of "Valley of the Dolls," dies.

Sept. 22, 1974: Sonny returns to the airwaves with *The Sonny Comedy Revue*. Show stars Sally Struthers who sings "In the Mood," Howard Cossell who does a commentary of the fight between David and Goliath, the Jackson 5 who sing "Life of the Party," and Miss Teenage America Lori Lei Matsukawa.

Sept. 23, 1974: Robbie McIntosh of The Average White Band dies of a heroin overdose at a North Hollywood party — apparently he mistakes heroin for cocaine.

October 1974: *Monty Python's Flying Circus*, an outrageously brilliant comedy show from England, airs on PBS.

Oct. 8, 1974: President Ford distributes WIN buttons, which stand for "Whip Inflation Now."

Oct. 13, 1974: Ed Sullivan dies.

Oct. 30, 1974: Muhammad Ali regains the world heavyweight championship by knocking out George Foreman in Zaire.

November 1974: Roxy Music's LP "Country Life" with controversial cover of semi-nude women is censored in the United States with opaque green shrink-wrap.

November 1974: *Earthquake*, a movie about an earthquake centered in Los Angeles, is released utilizing a new sound technology called "Sensurround," a system using loud, low decibel stereo sound to "shake" the theater.

November 1974: Bob Fosse's film biography of Lenny Bruce, *Lenny*, is released. It stars Dustin Hoffman.

Nov. 13, 1974: *Trial of Billy Jack* is released.

Nov. 14, 1974: Nuclear fuel facility laboratory technician Karen Silkwood is killed in an auto crash outside of Oklahoma City, Oklahoma. She is on her way to meet with a *New York Times* reporter and union official to document Kerr-McGee Nuclear Corporation's gross mishandling of plutonium and related products.

Nov. 16, 1974: "Whatever Gets You Thru The Night" by John Lennon and the Plastic Ono Nuclear Band hits #1 on *Billboard's* Top 40.

December 1974: Among films released this month are *The Towering Inferno*, and *Young Frankenstein*.

Dec. 2, 1974: House leader Wilbur Mills and stripper Fanny Fox are discovered to be having an affair.

Dec. 3, 1974: Pioneer 11 heads toward Saturn after surviving a pass within 26,000 miles of Jupiter.

Dec. 12, 1974: Citing creative differences and wanting to pursue a solo career, Mick Taylor leaves The Rolling Stones.

Dec. 12, 1974: Governor Jimmy Carter of Georgia begins bid for 1976 presidential election.

Dec. 26, 1974: Jack Benny dies.

Dec. 29, 1974: *The Sonny Comedy Revue* ends its run on TV. Last show stars Karen Valentine (whose comedy show takes over the slot), Clifton Davis of TV show *That's My Mama*, and Carrie McDowall.

1975

Jan. 1, 1975: Jury convicts H.R. Haldeman, John N. Mitchell, John D. Ehrlichman, and Robert C. Mardian of cover-up charges in connection with the Watergate break-in.

Jan. 5, 1975: VP. Nelson Rockefeller heads a commission to investigate charges of illegal domestic spying by the CIA.

Jan. 7, 1975: A Led Zeppelin concert is canceled by Boston Mayor after fans cause $30,000 worth of damage while waiting to buy tickets.

Jan. 12, 1975: ABC-TV airs *The Court Martial of Lt. William Calley*. The dramatization stars Tony Busante as Calley, who had been charged under military justice with pre-meditated murder of at least 70 Vietnamese civilians who had been living in the hamlet of My Lai in March 1968.

Jan. 17, 1975: *The Jeffersons* premieres on CBS-TV. A spin-off of *All in the Family*, the black family leaves the Queens, New York neighborhood of the Bunkers for "a deluxe apartment in the sky" and the good life on the east side of Manhattan.

Jan. 17, 1975: Robert Blake premieres in the TV series *Baretta* on ABC-TV. The show is about a lone wolf detective who has little regard for standard police practice. In first episode, he tries to nail down the hoodlum who killed his girlfriend.

Jan. 18, 1975: Barry Manilow's "Mandy" hits #1 in *Billboard's* Top 40.

Jan. 21, 1975: John Dean gets $300,000 for book rights to tell his side of Watergate.

Jan. 24, 1975: Larry Fine of "The Three Stooges" dies.

Feb. 7, 1975: Dept. of Labor reports the highest unemployment rate since 1942 (8.2%).

Feb. 11, 1975: Margaret Thatcher becomes first woman elected to head Britain's Conservative party.

Feb. 14, 1975: Judge rules that "The Mickey Mouse Club Theme Song" cannot be used as background music for an orgy scene in *The Life and Times of Xaviera Hollander*, (author of the Happy Hooker).

Feb. 21, 1975: David Bowie releases "Young Americans/Suffragette City" single.

Feb. 21, 1975: Watergate conspirators John Mitchell, H.R. Haldeman, John Erlichman, and Robert Mardian are sentenced up to eight years each in prison.

Feb. 28, 1975: American Motors Corporation introduces a new car model, The Pacer.

March 5, 1975: Rocker Rod Stewart and actress Britt Eckland begin a highly publicized romance after meeting at a party given by Joni Mitchell in Los Angeles.

March 10, 1975: Pres. Thieu of S. Vietnam orders the evacuation of the Central Highlands after the fall of Ban Me Thuot.

March 26, 1975: The city of Hue in S. Vietnam is captured by N. Vietnamese.

March 26, 1975: Ken Russell's *Tommy*, which is based on the rock opera by The Who, premieres in London, England. *Tommy* also features Tina Turner and Elton John. The plot follows a mother abusing her handicapped son who overcomes his disabilities to become a champion pinball player or the "Pinball Wizard."

March 29, 1975: North Vietnam overtakes the city of Danang and moves towards the S. Vietnamese capital of Saigon.

April 1975: Miller Brewing Co. begins to market Miller Lite Beer.

April 5, 1975: Chiang Kai-shek dies.

April 5, 1975: The Department of Labor announces the highest unemployment since 1940 (8.7%).

1975 U.S. Pulls out

April 6, 1975: Dealing with the strange disappearances of planes and ships, between the area of Florida and Cuba, the book, *The Bermuda Triangle*, by Charles Berlitz, is #1 on the New York Times best seller list.

April 8, 1975: *The Godfather Part II* becomes the first film sequel to win best picture at Academy Awards.

April 15, 1975: Karen Ann Quinlan lapses into a coma after mixing alcohol and small doses of Librium and Valium.

April 16, 1975: Phnom Penh is captured by the Khmer Rouge rebels.

April 19, 1975: US. Bicentennial celebration includes re-enactment's of the battles of Lexington and Concord.

April 19, 1975: "The Hustle" by Van McCoy debuts on *Billboard* charts.

April 21, 1975: Pres. Thieu of S. Vietnam resigns.

April 30, 1975: Emergency helicopter evacuation removes last 1,000 American troops from Saigon. A few hours later, South Vietnamese government surrenders to the North Vietnam.

April 30, 1975: *Starsky and Hutch* pilot airs on ABC-TV. It stars Michael Glaser as Starsky and David Soul as Hutchinson (Hutch), two plain clothes police officers combing the city streets, fighting crime.

May 1975: After rejecting names like "The Portable Crushers" and "The Vague Dots," David Byrne, Tina Weymouth, and Chris Franz settle on "The Talking Heads," which they found in an old issue of *TV Guide*.

May 4, 1975: Moe Howard of "The Three Stooges" dies.

May 25, 1975: Alaska okays private use of marijuana.

June 1975: *Jaws*, centering on a massive great white shark attack off Martha's vineyard, and *Nashville*, centering on Robert Altman's comical great white attack on Nashville, are released.

June 4, 1975: The Rolling Stones become first band from the West to receive royalties from the Soviet Union.

June 21, 1975: "Love Will Keep Us Together" by the Captain and Tennille hits #1 on *Billboard's* Top 40.

June 28, 1975: Creator/host Rod Serling of *The Twilight Zone* and *Night Gallery* (two television dramas dealing with the strange and the macabre) dies of complications following open heart surgery.

June 30, 1975: Cher marries Gregg Allman, four days after she is divorced from Sonny Bono.

July 4, 1975: Hardware store owner Harold Keith Davisson seals a time capsule containing a Chevrolet Vega, a blue Kawasaki motorcycle, a Teflon frying pan, and a blue leisure suit among other things, to be opened in 2025.

July 5, 1975: Bad Company releases single, "Feel Like Makin' Love."

July 10, 1975: Cher files for divorce from Gregg Allman. She accuses him of moonlighting with an old flame.

July 17, 1975: US. and Soviet astronauts team up for Apollo/Soyuz space mission.

July 17, 1977: The self-help pep-talk book, *Your Erroneous Zones* by Wayne Dreyer, is #1 on the New York Times best-seller list.

of Viet Nam

Spirit of '76

July 24, 1975: Barbara Colby, the lovable hooker on *The Mary Tyler Moore Show* is shot to death shortly after taping her third episode of *Phyllis*. CBS declines to air Cloris Leachman's eulogy taped after the show aired feeling it would interfere with their laugh line-up.

July 31, 1975: Former teamster president Jimmy Hoffa is reported missing.

Aug. 11, 1975: Aerosmith's album, "Toys In The Attic," goes gold.

Aug. 16, 1975: Robert Plant of Led Zeppelin, his wife, and two children almost die in car wreck in Greece.

Aug. 20, 1975: Viking I blasts off for the planet Mars.

Aug. 26, 1975: TV series *Adam 12*, starring Kent McCord as Officer Reed and Martin Milner as Officer Malloy, ends after seven-year run.

Aug. 30, 1975: "Get Down Tonight" by Miami, Florida-based KC and the Sunshine Band hits #1 on *Billboard's* Top 40.

September 1975: *Space 1999* premieres as a syndicated series. Bearing a slight resemblance to Star Trek, Space 1999 revolves around the moon and moonbase Alpha which loses orbit and flies off into outer space.

September 1975: *Dog Day Afternoon* is released.

Sept. 5, 1975: Former Manson cult figure Lynette "Squeaky" Fromme attempts to kill President Ford in Sacramento. He is on his way to address the California Legislature about starting a national effort to curb violent crimes, including stricter gun control laws.

Sept. 8, 1975: *Sigmund and the Sea Monsters* premieres on Saturday morning TV. Disowned by his family for his inability to scare humans, Sigmund, a sea monster, leaves home and begins to wander along Cyprus Beach in California. The series centers around the efforts of two brothers to keep Sigmund's presence a secret and protect him from his family — who deviously scheme to retrieve him when emergencies arise that require his presence at home.

Sept. 9, 1975: First episode of *Welcome Back Kotter* airs on ABC-TV. Comic Gabe Kaplan stars as Gabe Kotter, a fledgling high school teacher saddled with classroom terrors who are much like he was when he attended the same school 10 years before. Marcia Strassman plays his wife Julie. In this opening episode, Gabe's academic misfits are challenged to a formal debate on the topic "Resolved: humans are basically aggressive." (The show is the national debut of John Travolta, who plays student Vinnie Barbarino.)

Sept. 18, 1975: Patricia Hearst is arrested in San Francisco.

Sept. 22, 1975: Sara Jane Moore attempts to assassinate President Ford.

Sept. 26, 1975: The film *The Rocky Horror Picture Show* premieres at the United Artists Westwood Theater in Los Angeles. Featuring Meatloaf and Susan Sarandon, this offbeat musical contains transvestitism, gore, and comedy.

Sept. 30, 1975: Home Box Office begins programming across US.

Oct. 9, 1975: Sean Ono Lennon is born.

Oct. 11, 1975: *NBC's Saturday Night* premieres. It is described in *TV Guide* as "a variety series that blends a range of musical acts with a topical brand of comedy." George Carlin is host for the opener, which features singers Janis Ian performing her hit "At Seventeen" and Billy Preston, plus three "new talent" segments. It also includes sketches and blackouts from regulars Albert Brooks, Jim Henson and the Muppets, and a repertory group: The Not Ready For Prime Time Players: Dan Ackroyd, John Belushi, Jane Curtin, Garrett Morris, Laraine Newman, and Gilda Radner. Lorne Michaels is the producer.

Oct. 16, 1975: The First Women's Bank opens in New York as first American bank committed to economic parity for women. Among its clients are Bloomingdales, CBS, Inc., *Ms. Magazine*, *The New York Times*, Miller Brewing Co., and Mobil Oil Corp.

Oct. 18, 1975: Simon and Garfunkel reunite on *Saturday Night Live* to play "My Little Town."

Oct. 25, 1975: The episode "Chuckles bites the dust" airs on *The Mary Tyler Moore Show*. Chuckles the clown, dressed as a peanut, is killed by a loose elephant. The news staff unsuccessfully try to fight back the laughter.

Oct. 27, 1975: *Time* and *Newsweek* covers feature Bruce Springsteen, session musician turned rock star.

November 1975: Roxy Music's "Love is a Drug" climbs to #30 in *Billboard's* Top 100.

November 1975: Betamax home video recording system by Sony first appears in America. People who wish to purchase it must buy it in a console that also includes a Sony color TV. Cost is up to $2,295.

November 1975: Ken Kesey's novel *One Flew Over the Cuckoo's Nest* is released as a movie.

Nov. 23, 1975: Cher and David Bowie sing duets of "Fame," "Can You Hear Me," and "Young Americans" on her TV. show.

Dec. 1, 1975: Bette Midler has an emergency appendectomy.

Dec. 7, 1975: Joey Stivic is born to Mike and Gloria on TV series *All in the Family*, a series depicting the life of a working class bigot and his neurotic wife.

Dec. 16, 1975: *One Day At A Time* premieres on CBS-TV. The series, which is set in Indianapolis, Indiana, depicts incidents in the lives of Ann Romano (Bonnie Franklin), a 34-year-old divorcee and her teenage daughters, Julie (Mackenzie Phillips) and Barbara (Valerie Bertinelli). Mark Hamill, later of Luke Skywalker/*Star Wars* fame, makes sporadic appearances as Harvey, the nephew of nosy, posturing apartment building superintendent Dwayne Schneider (Pat Harrington).

Dec. 17, 1975: Lynette "Squeaky" Fromme is sentenced to life in prison for her attempted assassination of President Ford.

Dec. 19, 1975: Ron Wood is named as new guitarist for The Rolling Stones.

1976

Jan. 1, 1976: Robert Plant walks again, after 6 months in a wheelchair, following an auto accident a year earlier in Greece.

Jan. 1, 1976: At midnight on New Year's Eve, the Liberty Bell, symbol of American independence, is moved to a new home. The famous cracked bell is carefully taken from Independence Hall in Philadelphia and moved 100 yards (91 meters) to a steel and glass pavilion in Independence Square.

Jan. 6, 1976: *Mary Hartman, Mary Hartman* premieres. Taking place in Fernwood Ohio, Louise Lasser plays a befuddled neurotic housewife, constantly drinking coffee, married to an All-American husband (impotent), with a 12 year old daughter. Stylized after every red-blooded American soap opera.

Jan. 10, 1976: "Convoy" by C.W. McCall hits #1 on *Billboard's* Top 40.

Jan. 10, 1976: Howlin' Wolf dies in Chicago.

Jan. 10, 1976: First lady Betty Ford makes a cameo appearance on *The Mary Tyler Moor Show*, as a tag to a story about Mary's trip to Washington DC. with her boss, Lou Grant.

Jan. 12, 1976: Agatha Christie, 85, British mystery writer, dies in England. Dame Agatha, author of over 100 books, was the creator of Hercule Poirot, one of the most popular characters in detective fiction. Her books have been translated into 103 languages.

Jan. 14, 1976: Jaime Sommers, girlfriend of the Six Million Dollar Man, is brought back to life after dying during the last season and is given her own TV series — *The Bionic Woman*.

Jan. 23, 1976: *Donny and Marie* premieres as a weekly variety hour of music, songs, and comedy sketches, hosted by Donny and Marie Osmond of the wholesome Osmond family. Regulars include Paul Lynde, The Osmond Brothers, and The Ice Vanities.

Jan. 31, 1976: Gary Wright's "Dream Weaver" climbs into *Billboard's* Top 40.

February 1976: Martin Scorcese's *Taxi Driver* is released.

Feb. 1, 1976: *Rich Man, Poor Man* premieres. A nine-part miniseries based on the novel by Irwin Shaw, the show follows the lives of the Jordache brothers: Rudy, the straight one who moves up the establishment ladder, and Tom, the troublemaker. The series, which is among the first miniseries innovations, simultaneously covers the changes in America from World War II through the mid-1960s.

Feb. 4, 1976: A severe earthquake, which registers 7.5 on the 9-point Richter scale, strikes Guatemala. More than 22,000 people lose their lives in the disaster, and about 74,000 are hurt. The quake is felt throughout the country as well as in neighboring Honduras and El Salvador.

Feb. 12, 1976: Actor Sal Mineo is murdered in Los Angeles at age 37. He is remembered for acting in films (*Rebel without a Cause*) and a 1957 Top 10 hit "Start Movin'."

Feb. 12, 1976: Soviet-backed forces in Angola claim victory.

Feb. 21, 1976: "Show Me The Way" by Peter Frampton is released as a single.

Feb. 29, 1976: The book *Helter Skelter* hits #1 on best seller list.

March 9, 1976: *Family* airs on ABC-TV, featuring incidents in the complex day-to-day lives of the Lawrences, a middle-income family of six living at 1230 Holland St. in Pasadena, California. Cast includes James Broderick, Sada Thompson, Meredith Baxter-Birney, Gary Frank, and Kristy McNichol.

March 20, 1976: Patricia Hearst, the daughter of publisher Randolph A. Hearst, is convicted in San Francisco of robbing a bank and using a firearm to commit the robbery.

March 21, 1976: Pilot for *Charlie's Angels* airs on ABC-TV depicting three women investigators working for a detective agency, given their orders by a man who they never see.

March 22, 1976: For the first time, representatives of Israel and the Palestine Liberation Organization (PLO) engage in a debate at the United Nations. Until then, Israel had boycotted all meetings of the Security Council at which representatives of the PLO were present.

March 24, 1976: President Gerald R. Ford calls for a government-supported campaign to vaccinate the entire population of the United States against a virus strain related to swine influenza. The strain is believed to be similar to the one that had caused the death of 20,000,000 people in the epidemic of 1918-19.

March 29, 1976: Elizabeth Taylor closes Academy Awards ceremony by leading a salute to the US. Bicentennial. *One Flew Over the Cuckoo's Nest* is the big winner.

March 31, 1976: New Jersey Supreme Court rules unanimously that Karen Ann Quinlan's father can request she be removed from a life sustaining respirator.

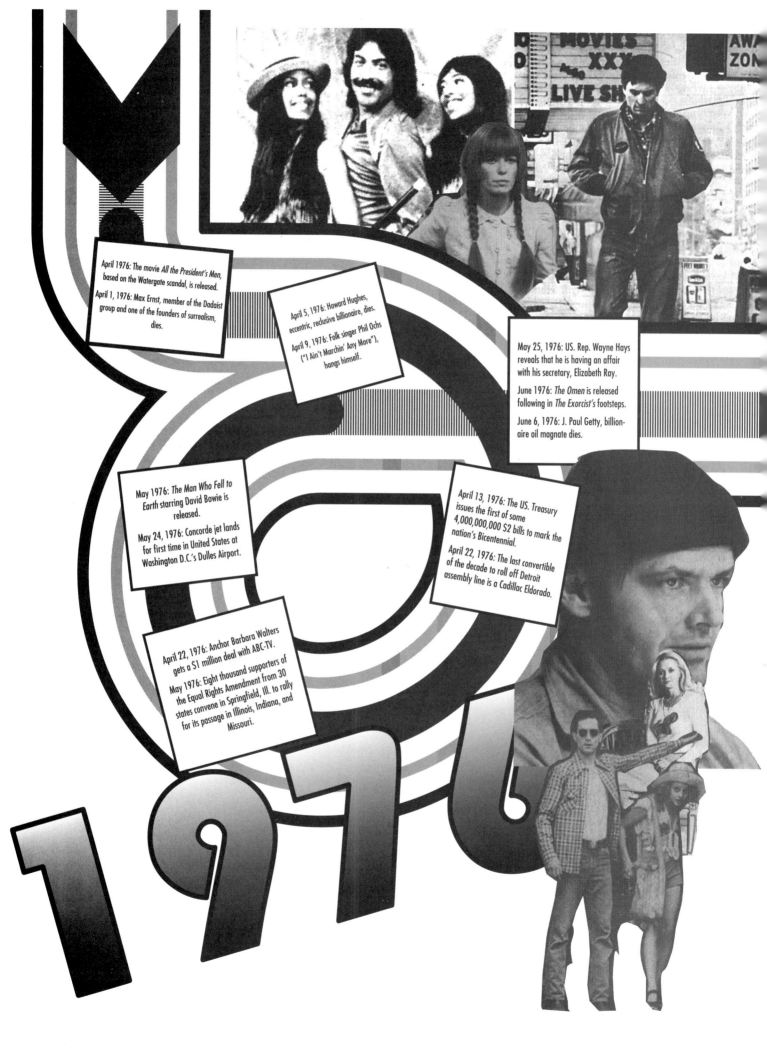

April 1976: The movie *All the President's Men*, based on the Watergate scandal, is released.

April 1, 1976: Max Ernst, member of the Dadaist group and one of the founders of surrealism, dies.

April 5, 1976: Howard Hughes, eccentric, reclusive billionaire, dies.

April 9, 1976: Folk singer Phil Ochs ("I Ain't Marchin' Any More"), hangs himself.

May 25, 1976: US. Rep. Wayne Hays reveals that he is having an affair with his secretary, Elizabeth Ray.

June 1976: *The Omen* is released following in *The Exorcist's* footsteps.

June 6, 1976: J. Paul Getty, billionaire oil magnate dies.

May 1976: *The Man Who Fell to Earth* starring David Bowie is released.

May 24, 1976: Concorde jet lands for first time in United States at Washington D.C.'s Dulles Airport.

April 13, 1976: The US. Treasury issues the first of some 4,000,000,000 $2 bills to mark the nation's Bicentennial.

April 22, 1976: The last convertible of the decade to roll off Detroit assembly line is a Cadillac Eldorado.

April 22, 1976: Anchor Barbara Walters gets a $1 million deal with ABC-TV.

May 1976: Eight thousand supporters of the Equal Rights Amendment from 30 states convene in Springfield, Ill. to rally for its passage in Illinois, Indiana, and Missouri.

1976

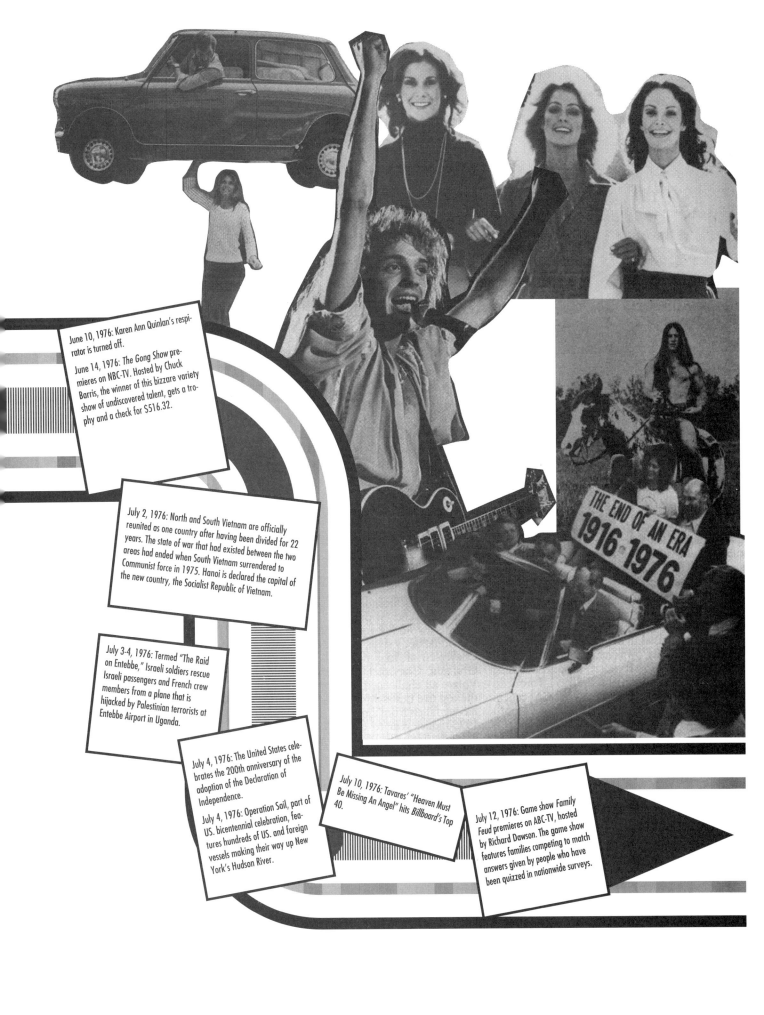

June 10, 1976: Karen Ann Quinlan's respirator is turned off.

June 14, 1976: The Gong Show premieres on NBC-TV. Hosted by Chuck Barris, the winner of this bizzare variety show of undiscovered talent, gets a trophy and a check for S516.32.

July 2, 1976: North and South Vietnam are officially reunited as one country after having been divided for 22 years. The state of war that had existed between the two areas had ended when South Vietnam surrendered to Communist force in 1975. Hanoi is declared the capital of the new country, the Socialist Republic of Vietnam.

July 3-4, 1976: Termed "The Raid on Entebbe," Israeli soldiers rescue Israeli passengers and French crew members from a plane that is hijacked by Palestinian terrorists at Entebbe Airport in Uganda.

July 4, 1976: The United States celebrates the 200th anniversary of the adoption of the Declaration of Independence.

July 4, 1976: Operation Sail, part of US. bicentennial celebration, features hundreds of US. and foreign vessels making their way up New York's Hudson River.

July 10, 1976: Tavares' "Heaven Must Be Missing An Angel" hits Billboard's Top 40.

July 12, 1976: Game show Family Feud premieres on ABC-TV, hosted by Richard Dawson. The game show features families competing to match answers given by people who have been quizzed in nationwide surveys.

THE END OF AN ERA 1916-1976

July 12-15, 1976: Jimmy Carter clinches Democratic nomination for US president, with running-mate Walter Mondale.

July 17, 1976: Heart releases the single "Magic Man."

July 20, 1976: Viking I, an unmanned US. spacecraft, completes its voyage to Mars and places a robot lander on the planet. The lander begins its search for signs of life.

July 21-24, 1976: A mysterious ailment later called "legionnaire's disease" kills 29 people attending American Legion convention in Philadelphia, Pennsylvania.

Aug. 8, 1976: Boston releases its debut album, "Boston."

Aug. 11, 1976: The *Welcome Back Kotter* theme song by John Sebastian hits #1 on *Billboard's* Top 40.

Aug. 13, 1976: The Clash perform their first concert in London, England.

Aug. 16-19, 1976: Gerald Ford and Sen. Robert Dole win Republican nomination for US President.

Aug. 24, 1976: Two Soviet cosmonauts return safely to earth after a 48-day research program aboard the orbiting Salyut 5 space station.

Aug. 29,1976: Annissa Jones who played Buffy on *Family Affair* dies of a drug overdose from Quaaludes and alcohol at the age of eighteen.

Aug. 30, 1976: The volcano, La Soufriere erupts on the French Caribbean island of Guadeloupe.

Aug. 31, 1976: Pilot for TV series *Alice* airs on CBS-TV. Linda Lavin plays the title role in this show about a widowed mother who is working as a waitress in Mel's Diner in Phoenix, Arizona while waiting to resume her career as a piano-bar singer. The comedy is based on the 1974 Martin Scorsese movie *Alice Doesn't Live Here Any More.*

Aug. 31, 1976: Judge rules that George Harrison subconsciously plagiarized the Chiffon's "He's So Fine" in writing his "My Sweet Lord."

Sept. 3, 1976: The Viking II lander touches down on the plain of Utopia on Mars.

Sept. 9, 1976: Chinese Communist Party Chairman Mao Tse-tung, 82, dies. Mao was a founder of the Chinese Communist Party and had been the leader of the People's Republic of China since its creation in 1949.

Sept. 16, 1976: The dispute over whether women should be allowed to become priests of the Episcopal Church ends with a provision that ordination to the priesthood applies equally to women and men.

Sept. 17, 1976: Pilot for *The Love Boat*, a show that features romantic entanglements aboard a cruise ship, airs on ABC-TV; guest stars for this two-hour extravaganza include Tom Bosley, Cloris Leachman, Don Adams, Florence Henderson, Karen Valentine, and Gabe Kaplan.

Sept. 29, 1976: Richard Nixon sells memoirs for $2 million.

October 1976: *Car Wash* is released.

Oct. 3, 1976: *Quincy* premieres on NBC-TV. Jack Klugman plays the title role—a Los Angeles medical examiner who discovers that catching killers is more exciting than dissecting their victims.

Oct. 8, 1976: EMI signs The Sex Pistols.

Oct. 16, 1976: Rick Dees "Disco Duck" hits #1 on *Billboard's* Top 40.

November 1976: *Network* is released.

1976

Nov. 4, 1976: Jimmy Carter narrowly defeats Gerald Ford in US presidential election.

Nov. 12, 1976: American artist, Alexander Calder dies at age 78. Calder was known for his mobiles (sculptures with parts that can be set in motion by air currents or by touching).

Nov. 14, 1976: Keith Reif of The Yardbirds dies after being electrocuted on stage.

Nov. 18,1976: Man Ray, member of the Dadaist and Surrealist groups, dies in Paris.

Nov. 18, 1976: Richard Hell and the Voidoids hold premiere concert at CBGB's.

Nov. 19, 1976: Patricia Hearst is released on $1.5 million bail.

Nov. 25, 1976: The Band holds its last concert, *The Last Waltz*, at San Francisco's Winterland. Director Martin Scorsese is on-hand to film the event.

Dec. 1, 1976: The newly independent country of Angola is admitted to the United Nations.

Dec. 4, 1976: Benjamin Britten, 63, British composer, dies. Among his best-known works are *Death in Venice* and the mass *War Requiem*.

Dec. 4, 1976: Tommy Bolin of Deep Purple dies from heroin overdose.

Dec. 4, 1976: Bob Marley and his manager are shot at Marley's home in Kingston, Jamaica.

Dec. 16, 1976: The swine-flu vaccination program, sponsored by the US. Government, is halted because at least 94 people suffered a form of paralysis. An investigation begins to find out if there is a link between the paralysis and the flu vaccine.

1977

Jan. 14, 1977: Pilot for *Fantasy Island* airs on ABC-TV. It is a show about an exotic island where $50,000 buys the dreams of three guests. Guest stars include Bill Bixby, who plays a lonely World War II vet yearning to relive a brief wartime romance with a woman named Francesca (played by Sandra Dee); also starring Peter Lawford, Victoria Principal, and Dick Sargent. Their host is Mr. Roarke, played by Ricardo Mantalban.

Jan. 17, 1977: US. ends its 10-year moratorium on capitol punishment as Gary Gilmore is executed by firing squad.

Jan. 21, 1977: President Jimmy Carter pardons most Vietnam War draft evaders who number some 10,000.

Jan. 28, 1977: Comedian Freddie Prinze, star of TV's *Chico and the Man*, commits suicide at the age of 22.

Jan. 30, 1977: The TV series *Roots* sets new records. The series about slaves coming to the New World is based on the best selling novel by Alex Halley.

Feb. 5, 1977: Elvis Presley's "Moody Blue" hits *Billboard's* Top 40.

Feb. 15, 1977: "Rumors" LP by Fleetwood Mac is released.

Feb. 27, 1977: Keith Richard is busted for heroin in Toronto.

March 1977: Punkdom's "Romeo and Juliet," Sid Vicious and Nancy Spungen, meet in London.

March 9, 1977: US. Food and Drug Administration announces a ban on the use of saccharin in food, soft drinks, chewing gum, and toothpaste after a Canadian study links its intake with bladder cancer in laboratory rats.

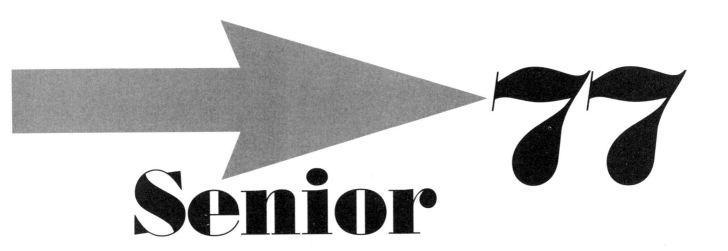

1977

March 15, 1977: *Three's Company* airs on ABC-TV. It stars Suzanne Somers, Joyce DeWitt, and John Ritter and focuses on the trio's struggle to maintain strictly platonic relationships.

March 19, 1977: Last regular season episode of *The Mary Tyler Show* airs. The show, which had featured the antics in the newsroom of WJM-TV in Minneapolis, Minnesota, starred Moore as Mary Richards, Ed Asner as Lou Grant, Ted Knight as Ted Baxter, Gavin MacLeod as Murray Slaughter, Betty White as Sue Ann Nivens, and Georgia Engel as Georgette.

March 22, 1977: Lily Tomlin makes her Broadway debut in *Lily Tomlin On Stage*.

April 1977: Woody Allen's *Annie Hall* is released.

April 16, 1977: David Soul's "Don't Give Up On Us" hits #1 on *Billboard's* Top 40.

April 21, 1977: *Annie* opens on Broadway.

April 26, 1977: New York discotheque Studio 54 opens. Known for it's selective entrance policies, similar to the TV game show *Lets Make a Deal*.

May 1977: George Lucas mega-sci-fi hit *Star Wars* is released.

May 1977: Apple II computer is introduced for $1,195. It has 16K of memory.

May 11, 1977: Chlorofluorocarbons are outlawed as propellants in spray cans.

May 21, 1977: Jerry Hall dumps Bryan Ferry to live with Mick Jagger.

May 28, 1977: Graduation ceremonies are held for the seniors at Robert E. Lee High School.

June 20, 1977: First oil from Alaska pipeline flows.

July 13, 1977: Amidst a heat wave, New York City experiences blackout caused by alleged electric storm. It lasts 25 hours.

July 22, 1977: Stiff Records releases Elvis Costello's first LP, *My Aim is True*. It includes the song "Alison," which is released as a single.

July 31, 1977: Variety show hosted by The Starland Vocal Band premieres on CBS-TV; show lasts six episodes.

Aug. 10, 1977: David "Son of Sam" Berkowitz is captured.

Aug. 12, 1977: The first space shuttle is tested.

Aug. 16, 1977: Elvis Presley dies. President Jimmy Carter responds by saying, "Elvis Presley's death deprives our country of a part of itself. He was unique and irreplaceable." Presley's death is first reported due to a heart attack, but later to a drug overdose.

Aug. 19, 1977: Groucho Marx dies.

Sept. 13, 1977: *Soap* premieres on ABC-TV. A satire of afternoon soap operas, the show depicts the lives of two sisters and their families: the wealthy Jessica Tate (Cathryn Damon) and her husband Chester (Robert Mandan), and the not-so-rich Mary Campbell (Katherine Helmond) and her husband Burt (Richard Mulligan).

Sept. 17, 1977: Marc Bolan of T Rex dies in car crash.

Sept. 26, 1977: Laker Airways charges amazingly low price of $102 from London to New York.

Sept. 28, 1977: Bing Crosby and David Bowie record "Peace on Earth," but Crosby dies before it is seen or released.

Senior year

Sept. 29, 1977: Andy Warhol interviews Mick Jagger, Keith Richards, and Ron Wood for *Interview* Magazine.

Oct. 14, 1977: Bing Crosby dies.

Oct. 15, 1977: "You Light Up My Life" peaks at #1 on *Billboard's* Top 40.

Oct. 20, 1977: Ronnie Van Zant and Steve Gaines from Lynyrd Skynyrd die in plane crash en route from Greenville, South Carolina to a concert in Baton Rouge, Louisiana. Their rented single engine plane runs out of gas.

Oct. 22, 1977: Queen releases "We Are the Champions/We Will Rock You."

Oct. 24, 1977: *Village Voice* critic says in review of recently released David Lynch film, *Eraserhead,* that it's "not a movie I'd drop acid for."

Oct. 29, 1977: Meat Loaf releases forthcoming chart smasher *Bat Out Of Hell*.

Nov. 5, 1977: Band leader Guy Lombardo dies of a heart attack in Houston, Texas.

Nov. 7, 1977: *Lindsay Wagner— Another Side of Me* airs on ABC-TV. The star of *The Bionic Woman* stars in a variety special that explores her favorite fantasies including a spoof of "the Perils of Pauline," an aquatic production in which she swims, and a number in which she sings with Paul Anka and her husband, Michael Brandon.

Nov. 19, 1977: Egyptian president Anwar Sadat becomes first Arab leader to visit Israel.

December 1977: *Saturday Night Fever* and *The Goodbye Girl* are released.

Dec. 10, 1977: The Sex Pistols release *Never Mind The Bollocks, Here's The Sex Pistols* on Warner Brothers Records.

Dec. 24, 1977: The Bee Gee's "How Deep Is Your Love" hits #1 on *Billboard's* Top 40.

Dec. 24, 1977: The Ramones' "Rocket to Russia" hits the charts.

Dec. 25, 1977: Film great Charlie Chaplin dies at his Swiss estate.

DAZED & CONFUSED

19. Move slow... it takes a while for everybody to get to the pep rally — ample time to blow a reefer. Use a smokeless pen pipe™.

20. Play an instrument in band class. That way, you can sign up to use the practice rooms, or should I say opium dens...

21. Go on as many field trips as you can; (as if you didn't want to anyway). It's harder for them to keep track of you, you know, so it's easier for you to split/slip/spleef off.

22. Run for student council, so you have the temporary building all to yourself.

23. Use any religious holiday you can think of to get out of class. Leave and worship the Red-Budded One.

24. In Home-Ekkk, stash your weed in the oregano spice can. Cook spaghetti with lots of "spice."

25. Or, in Home-Bleckkk, light spaghetti strands on the stove to cover up the smell of the pot you just smoked OR start a grease fire so you can smoke some major budd-age.

26. Smoke, buy more, smoke some more, all in the safety of the Smoking Section. (Be sure to keep a regular cigarette burning.)

27. Fire alarms for when you're really jonesing.

28. Join the F.F.A. (Future Farmers of America), smoke out in the animal trailers where the stench will hide anything.

29. At the pep rally wait for everyone to clap for the cheerleaders, then take a hit off that three-foot bong.

30. Light up while waiting for the school bus.

31. Become an Audio/Visual (A/V) nerd, this gives you free access to wander the hallways. Smoke in the closet where they store all the film and slide projectors.

32. Start a cafeteria food fight. This is a good diversion to do a quick one-hit.

33. Join the track team and smoke weed while running long distance.

34. Be a hall monitor. Cops get away with murder.

35. Find out which teachers smoke pot... Eventually you'll be in one of their classes. Use it against them, sell them some pot, or steal their diaries for blackmail - usually found in the top drawer of their desk. (Go see Ms. Stroud's classroom.)

36. Get the back seat on the school bus — the driver can't see you and the people who sit in the back don't care if you smoke anyway (you'll probably have to share...).

37. Create a parking lot diversion. Take turns having someone burn rubber so the parking lot narc will chase after them. Meanwhile, see how much pot you and your friends can smoke before he makes it back to your side of the parking lot.

38. Skip class, break into the teacher's lounge, toke yourself silly.

39. In Health class, sit in the back row when they have the police come in and lecture you on drugs. They pass around a box with a couple of joints in it, so you can see what marijuana looks like. Roll a couple of fake joints before class. Exchange. Ask to go to the bathroom.

40. Join some kind of after-school club. It's like having the play ground all to yourself.

41. Shop class is the time to light-up; the classrooms are huge, and you can always tell if your teacher is really involved in some project on the other side of the room.

42. In Journalism they usually let you go anywhere in school with your press pass; you know — freedom of the press...

43. Ditch class when the kitchen crew is

gone after lunch, so you're in the best spot when you get the munchies...

44. Automatic pipes, need I say more? Lighter, stash, bowl all in one. Smokeless, coolness!

45. Go into the basement during lunch to explore all the nooks and crannies while smoking bowl after bowl (even more fun with member of the opposite sex, or your pot dealer...).

46. Excuse yourself from class using any obscure religious holiday (this works great to get your other friends out of class too). Smoke on the way to church, temple, synagogue, Y.M.C.A. , pool hall...

47. Give your teacher an excuse to walk out of the room. Example: start throwing up and run out of the room, calling for help. (Your friends will spot you a joint later).

48. Get to know the long-haired janitor. Follow him to his "secret" spot.

49. Find a way up to the roof. Bring lounge chairs, kick back and relax. When's the last time you saw the principal trying to make siege on the school roof?

50. Light up in class. Advantages: You don't have to go to school so you can smoke whenever you want, and you don't need money in jail because you can trade cigarettes for weed. Disadvantages: Suspension, a life sentence (for killing someone over a pinner), heroin addiction.

51. Climb into the drainage ditches or steam tunnels and smoke.

52. Push out the fake sound tiles in the hallway ceiling then have someone boost you up there. Crawl around and explore while roasting that doobie.

53. Join the swim team. You can smoke in the locker room after school and get rid of the reek when you go swimming.

54. Call in a bomb threat; drag your feet while leaving so you can get lost in the crowd that smokes the weed.

55. Smoke underneath the cars in automotive class.

56. Kiss your coach's ass — "volunteer" to wash the towels after gym, this gives you time to light up and find possible future fuel for blackmail.

57. Find the room with the main power box; smoke while contemplating your next move...

58. After seeing "Roots," claim it's your natural birth-right as a native American Indian (or whatever) to smoke marijuana whenever and wherever you want.

59. Do one-hits while dissecting fetal pigs in biology. The formaldehyde overpowers the skunk weed, 2 to 1. (While you're at it, cut off one of the front feet to use for a roach-clip later).

60. Always light up when using a bunsen burner.

61. In Socio-EcoPlumbing class, weld two pieces of copper pipe together, insert window screen, light and share with class.

62. Have a "seizure," tell the nurse it was an epileptic fit brought on by glaucoma and that you have a joint in your "medicine bag."

63. Smoke under the stairs between classes. The smoke will rise and you'll have an escape route at the bottom of the stairs.

64. On windy days, torch-up between buildings.

65. Usually in any foreign language class they have a day where you get to eat some of the food from that country. Take Moroccan; the curry smell will eat up the smell of any hash. Bring brownies for dessert. If questioned, say you thought brownies originated in the Middle East.

66. Have one of your friends "flip out" on acid. Tell your teacher you need to take them outside for some fresh air, so you can "talk

them down." Ditch class; smoke a joint in the parking lot.

67. In Astronomy class, complain that you thought it was astrology class and your psychic advisor told you that it was alright to smoke pot during the rap session.

68. Have an anxiety attack so you can go see your councilor. If you're lucky, he/she will want to "rap" with you. Casually take out a joint and start puffing. They'll think you're under a lot of pressure; most likely, they'll make you put it out. But that's usually after you've had a couple drags.

69. Steal a book of hall passes; this gives you access to the whole school.

70. Jim Morrison is dead, and now Keith Moon. Wait till Elvis dies, then run out of the room screaming "Dead! Dead! They're all Dead!" in between buildings and torch up, in memorial.

71. In debate class take a stand: because of the Energy Crisis it's a waste of money to be attending school that day. Walk out proudly, showing your true colors: red (hair), white (smoke), & blue (lungs).

72. Seduce Ms. Stroud (or any other young, nubile "instructor") this guarantees your "liberation" to leave her/his class at any time.

73. Go to class sporting some horrible bodily odor. After offending everyone in class, they'll probably make you leave. If that doesn't work, soil yourself.

74. Do one-hits in the back of the class. Drop a stink bomb to cover the odor.

75. Make loud accusations that your teacher is a known member of the SLA; the louder you

are, the faster they'll run to the front office for help. Light up while waiting for the principal to take you to detention hall.

76. On Washington's birthday start puffing on a joint in History class while ranting that your forefathers smoked pot and it's your right, too. If they don't let you, scream at the top of your lungs that they're un-American.

77. Bet your friend a joint that they can't spell out "SHELLOIL" on a pocket calculator. When they give up, punch in the number 71077345 and flip the calculator over. Toke the ganja in the slide rule repair department.

78. Put a giant screen in your alto sax during Music class. Duct-tape all the holes shut. Light, suck.

79. Form the longest lunch line possible with all your friends. Light up and pass a joint down the lunch line (speed is an important factor here). If questioned about the aroma, look stupid and point to the kitchen.

80. Try out for the cheerleaders whether you can lead cheers or not (or if you're a boy or a girl). Regularly fall down and sprain your ankle so you can watch them from a good smoking distance.

81. Get on the photo journalism staff and demand they send you over to Vietnam, where the real pot is.

82. Get in with the Future Nurses Club — they're always a good connection.

83. Any adventure club usually goes on trips and gets you out of class for a couple of days. They're also usually run by ex-hippies.

84. Become sensitive, shy, and confused. This will dupe any teacher into cutting you 100% slack, which is always your ticket to freedom, brother.

85. Volunteer to stack books for the librarian. Disappear in the stacks and puff away. If questioned, blame it on gas — they'll never know the difference.

86. Drink a fifth of bourbon before you get to school; by second period, they'll throw you out of class (if you don't throw up in class). If your coordination is still together, try to fire up that weed on the way home from school.

87. Freak out in class, screaming "I don't want to be eligible for the draft!" Run out of the room, towards the opium den of your choice; it will take them a joint's worth of time for them to find you.

88. Volunteer for the job of raising the school flag in the morning, so you can salute the colors as they follow a cloud of smoke.

89. Lock yourself in the room where the faculty hangs their coats. Exhale through their jackets.

90. Take typing class and type yourself a note from your mother, excusing you from that period (or the next period) and have your friend sign your mom's John Hancock.

91. In automotive class, have your weed stashed under the seat of your mini bike. Toke up when welding on your muffler.

92. Smoke a joint before school starts. Exhale into a big glass jar with a lid, stash the jar in your locker, take hits off it in between classes.

93. Before school, make "ice tea" out of your pot. Keep it in the thermos of your "Partridge Family" lunch box.

94. At the Formal Dance, have a joint stashed in the knot of your tie. Sneak off into a darkened corner and light.

95. Try out for the Talent Show. Do something patriotic with sparklers, there'll be so much smoke that nobody can see that joint next to the sparkler in your mouth.

96. During the "Halloween Dance" dress up as a Hippy™ smoking a fake joint. Make it out of a rolling paper, tobacco, and some flour. Blow through it to make the flour puff out like smoke. Switch it with a real joint when the coast is clear.

97. Join the pep club. Request huge bonfires for every pep rally. Stuff the pile of wood with tons of paper for extra smoke. Roll lots of pin joints and stand in the second row.

98. Act stupid so you can get thrown into a "special-ed." class. Usually the teacher is worse off than the students, and you're "special" — no matter what you do (or smoke).

99. Get a fog machine, like the one KISS uses. Light up in class. If they suspect you're smoking some weed, blast 'em with your fog machine. Use it for cover when you run out the door.

100. Set your school on fire. The thick, billowing clouds of smoke will hide the reek of weed, 100% guaranteed.

101. Repeat all of the above at school tomorrow.

Watergate, continued from p.46

all, were men who did terrible things and told enormous lies on television to cover their rear ends.

It's taken over a year of Gerald Ford bonking his head and boring the pants off everyone for me to realize that presidents can also be regular guys. We're being taught that Watergate proves that the system works, apparently because Congress didn't have to surround the White House with US Marines and force Nixon to leave at gun point. But I'm not so sure. In fact, I feel cheated. The constitution Ford swore to uphold and defend specifically states that pardons do not apply to impeachable offenses. But they let him get away with it.

There was a lot of talk about how the nation was spared the awful trauma of Nixon's trial before the Senate. The nation was also spared the logical climax of the greatest constitutional drama since the Civil War, and future presidents were spared the full impact of the lesson. Watergate should have been a banshee howling down the next fifty or one hundred years to leaders facing criminal temptation: "DON'T EVEN THINK ABOUT IT!." Ford's pardon muffled that cry. Now, Nixon is nursing his sore leg out at San Clemente while his lawyers battle for control of the White House tapes. Only a small part of them were released to the public. I wonder if we'll ever know everything he did.

Bicentennial Means to Us, continued from page 42

The details of the contingency plan were transmitted by the CIA to the 5/12 Committee, a super-secret group of policy makers whose job it is to approve or disapprove all major covert operations. Reportedly, the plan was not approved, and didn't go forward... Although...

A memo was written by Secretary of Defense McNamara directing the CIA to prepare contingency plans for the "elimination" of Mr. Castro. A later note, in Attorney General Robert Kennedy's handwriting, allegedly says "have this followed up vigorously".

In testimony to the Rockefeller Commission, a former FBI agent, Robert A. Mahue (later an aid to Howard Hughes) recruited the help of two underworld gangsters, Sam Giancana and his lieutenant on the west coast, John Roselli.

Giancana was set up at the Fountainbleu Hotel in Miami Beach Florida by the CIA in 1960 to handle the operation. The operation being an arrangement with a Cuban assassin to poison Premier Castro, his brother Raul, and Che Guevara, the Cuban revolutionary.

Cuban Deputy Premier Carlos Rodrigues claims that over 100 attempts have been made on Castro's life including "bombing, shooting and poison." Rodrigues claims that many of the attempts were made by groups in Cuba, organized or aided by the CIA. David A. Phillips, resigned Chief of Latin American affairs, confirms one attempt.

According to Richard Cain, former Chicago police officer (assistant and driver to Giancana), although they recruited gangsters and trained for the operation, the plot was not carried out. Later, Richard Cain would be gunned down, in a "gangland style" shooting in 1973.

Meanwhile, at FBI headquarters, Mr. Hoover received information of the whole plot, and was concerned that Mr. Giancana "could blackmail the United States Government".

During this whole investigation, on June 19th 1975 at around 10pm, Giancana was found in his living room, shot seven times in the head and neck, with one of the shots fired directly into his mouth (a gangsters way of showing that people who talk to grand juries don't live too long).

It was a pro hit, with witnesses saying that they saw two men wearing dark suits outside of the house (they were later identified as law enforcement officials, but there was no explanation of who they were, and why they were there in the first place).

Was it the CIA, the FBI, or the Mafia who put an end to Sam Giancana's life?

Upon further investigation, we posed another question: Where the heck was Dan Rowen? Could he have been the trigger man? He had a motive; his love affair was broken up because of a jealous boyfriend who probably wanted him out of the way.

We tried to reach him using my mom's phone, but he wasn't available for comment.

Upon reflecting about "What the Bicentennial Means to me", and after reviewing the past actions of how our country became the "great" nation that it is today, we just wonder whether it will it take another two hundred years to correct our corrupt government.

A somber moment for angst riddled freshman Carol "Tinsel Pout" Davenport. Her poem "New Moon Phonetap" garnered rave reviews in both homeroom and band. Here she is working on a piece tentatively titled "Elegy to Recess."

and disguised them by stashing a couple of Playboys under the mattress, in the back of the closet, and everywhere else they would look. (always give them something to find.) In the meantime I turned my three-foot bong into a tube/lava-like lamp (with the light bulb in the bong and the cord coming out of the bowl). It looked cool. The bullet went next to my bb-gun, and the smoke stones went in the turtle tank, below the plastic palm tree.

That wasn't too hard, but what I really wanted to do was smoke in privacy. So I got some incense — Opium and Black Love™ — and rolled-up a towel next to the crack at the bottom of the door, stuffing my "butterflies of love" t-shirt in the crack at the top of the door. That way no smoke would creep out into the living room, where they were watching TV.

Next, after lighting a couple of cones of Black Love™ incense and cracking the windows, (but not too much — I didn't want the smoke creeping around the house back into the front windows...,) I rolled a cool 2-paper joint in my deluxe chrome Rizla+™ luxury roller.

I was stoked! This time I knew it was going to work! No more creeping out the window for me. As I was halfway through my fine jay of red-hair, I noticed the smoke was getting a little too thick, but I knew it was nothing that a few good blasts of Opium™ couldn't take away .

Smoking at home is really no problem when you're well prepared. A couple of drops of Visine™ to get the red out, some more incense, burning all your clothes, and blaming it all on your older sister, are all you need to know to get high at home. Always keep up with High Times™ to see if there's any new, cool things out there for securing your bedroom. Remember: follow some precautions and you're set to toke, toke, toke.

TV TALK TV TALK TV TALK TV TALK TV TALK TV TALK TV TALK
BY Simmone Kerr

Here's my list of fave T.V. shows and some of the people that made them great... and remember, your T.V. is always on.

1. Mary Tyler Moore-
   MTM herself, Sue Ann Niven (Betty White), Georgette (Georgia Engel)
2. Phyllis- Phyllis (Cloris Leachman)
3. Mannix- Peggy Fair (Gail Fischer)
4. Sanford and Son- Aunt Esther (LaWanda Page)
5. Rhoda- Rhoda (Valerie Harper), Brenda (Julie Kavner), Ida (Nancy Walker)
6. Sonny and Cher- Cher
7. Maude- Carol (Adrienne Barbeau), Maude (Beatrice Arthur)
8. Good Times- Florida (Esther Rolle)
9. All in the Family- Edith (Jean Stapleton)
10. Get Christie Love- Christie Love (Teresa Graves)
11. The Jeffersons- Florence (Marla Gibbs)
12. Barney Miller- Fish (Abe Vigoda), Nick Yemana (Jack Soo)
13. Partridge Family- Keith (David Cassidy), Laurie (Susan Dey)
14. My old fave The Mod Squad (Peggy Lipton)

True or False

1. As part of his effort to cover up the traces of the Watergate burglary, Gordon Liddy shredded $100 bills.

   T_____   F_____

2. Among the assignments given "Sedan Chair I" was stealing the shoes of opposition workers when they were left in the hotel halls to be polished.

   T_____   F_____

3. During the course of an investigation, Gordon Liddy once locked himself in the trunk of an automobile.

   T_____   F_____

4. Former-President Nixon had an intense dislike of ice cubes with holes in them.

   T_____   F_____

5. Tony Ulasewicz secretly investigated the Smothers Brothers.

   T_____   F_____

6. Chuck Colson commissioned a firm to design a ray gun that could erase the presidential tapes even as they lay in their vaults.

   T_____   F_____

7. Former-President Nixon used to have the air-conditioning in the White House turned up to full capacity so he could have fires in the fireplaces in the summer.

   T_____   F_____

8. Gordon Liddy's method of insuring that an attempted burglary of George McGovern's headquarters would not be noticed by passersby was to fire a bullet through a light in a nearby alleyway.

   T_____   F_____

9. After the capture of the Watergate burglars, Howard Hunt ordered Alfred Baldwin to remove the monitoring equipment from the Howard Johnson's motel across the street from the Watergate and "take it anywhere but to Mr. McCord's house." Baldwin then took the equipment to McCord's home.

   T_____   F_____

10. During one year of his administration, Richard Nixon met only once with his Secretary of Defense, Elliot Richardson, but held two personal, private meetings with a veterinarian when his dog, King Timahoe, had mange.

    T_____   F_____

ing in Portugal, Italy, India-not to mention right here in America, where the Presidency is now an appointive office-the Center for the Study of Democratic Institutions has failed. I used to get a futurist magazine called *Fields Within Fields*. Last year, I got a letter: *Fields Withing Fields* has temporarily suspended publication. Even the future's a turkey! Remember the old joke about how tomorrow has been canceled due to lack of interest?

It is not merely that the Faith has fallen on hard times. We are also being inundated with images of failure. Michael Corleone fails in *Godfather II*. We discover in *French Connection II* that Popeye Doyle became a cop because he was a failure in professional sports. Jack Nicholson has built a career on playing failures. America lines up to see Jack fail as a concert pianist, see Jack fail as a radio personality, see Jack fail as a private eye, see Jack fail as a TV reporter, see Jack fail as a wife murderer. At this very moment, half the population of Brentwood is simmering in Jacuzzis, trying new ways for Jack to fail on each other.

Ragtime, which tacitly proposes itself as the epic novel of American failure, comes along when we're clinging to the ledge and stamps on our knuckles. Thank you, E. L. Doctorow. *Nashville* tacitly proposes itself as the epic film of American failure. According to *The New York Review of Books* - and it ought to know - director Robert Altman is the *Zeitgeist*, "because he represents a certain failure of nerve." Cecil B. DeMille specialized in representing triumphal entries into temple cities; John Ford specialized in representing the awesome grandeur of the trek West; and Robert Altman specializes in representing a certain failure of nerve. And here's a coincidence-guess who's going to bring *Ragtime* to the big screen?

Sonny Bono's TV show fizzled, but that wasn't so bad, because last season 29 out of 44 new prime-time shows clinked. Don Rickles' TV career sounds like a Don Rickles roast of Don Rickles. George Harrison's tour was a mobile disaster area. The former mop-top failed to browbeat arena animals into devoting their lives to Lord Krishna. Now, if Lord Krishna were a *pop wine*.... John Lennon *looks* like a failure. He can still get an occasional single on the radio, but then he shows up in a floppy beret and a white scarf, looking for all the world like a guy who lives out of two shopping bags and plays the cello on the street in front of Carnegie Hall for quarters. We're fortunate that so many rock stars of the Sixties killed themselves, because otherwise, our awareness would be crowded with even more high-energy failures. *Requiescat in pace*, Stephanie Edwards. And a word of thanks to McLean Stevenson for a manly, though failed, attempt to get her to admit on *The Tonight Show* that she was fired from *AM America*, which failed to provide any real competition for the *Today Show*, just like Sally Quinn and the *CBS Morning News*. Finally, of course, *AM America* itself failed.

Ah, yes, you will say, we decadent *cognoscenti* are being deluged with mythic images of failure, but the common folk -those who have fish decals on the backs of their cab-over campers, refer to beers as "cool ones" and dream in shades of avocado and mustard - surely these sturdy yeomen still cleave to success figures. Sure they do. Success figures like Evel Knievel. But as long as Evel succeeded at jumping his sickle over 100,000 midget gherkin jars or whatever, he was just another roadside

attraction. What made him hotter than fresh goat shit was when he began totaling. His miscarriage at the Snake River in the fall of 1974 was the most extensively publicized, highest-grossing nullity in the history of mass culture. We've come a long way from the days of Charles Lindbergh and Babe Ruth in our search for popular heroes. The surest way to become a mobile-household word these days is to pick out an implausible feat that nobody has yet been so self-destructive as to attempt, come on as belligerent and cocky as possible, fail ignominiously and blame your detractors. Kids these days are "playing Evel Knievel," riding bikes off board ramps-probably the first time small children have played at being someone who cripples himself for money.

Failure fetishism is good mind-rotting fun, but isn't it time we stopped jerking off over the pornography of failure and got naked with the real thing? Rather than simultaneously denying and worshipping failure, wouldn't it be easier on our nerves to come to terms with it? To force ourselves to admit that failure isn't really all that bad-any more than it's all that good?

The first thing we've got to understand is that sometimes being a failure is preferable to being a success. We live in a world of beautiful losers. Whom would you rather be marooned with on a desert island - Orson Welles or Blake Edwards? In a society that makes a Ray Kroc a peer of the realm for gracing the landscape with 3,186 golden arches, it shouldn't be surprising that the failures are more interesting than the successes.

I subscribe to a $300-a-year economic forecasting service put out by Muriel and Louis Hasbrouck, seers. You won't find that category in the Manhattan Yellow Pages between "Seeds & Bulbs-Whol." and "Seugros." But what else can you call people who wrote in 1972 that the major economic turning point of the rest of the 20th Century would come in mid-October 1973? The Hasbroucks postulate a wave of evolutionary trend change that has a periodicity of 36 years. They say that after the wave crested in 1966, we entered the phase known as the "time of trouble." It is this time of trouble that the prophet Bob Dylan was talking about in 1961 when he said a hard rain was gonna fall, that the prophet Norman Mailer was talking about in 1964 when he said a shitstorm was coming. The effect of the periodic time of trouble is evolutionary because any idea, any institution, any system that cannot resist or adapt to its onslaught falls by the wayside along with the pterodactyl, knights in shining armor, mercantilism and the 409-cubic-inch V8. The time of trouble is the painful but necessary prelude to what the Hasbroucks call the "cosmic house cleaning" that must take place so the decks will be clear for the next stage in the evolution of human consciousness and civilization, so that we'll have the space to create the tools that will get us through the next 36 years. And the cosmic Electrolux with which that house cleaning is performed is *failure*.

The Hasbroucks insist with the same cheerful assurance with which they predicted a climactic event for midsummer 1974 that the length of the time of trouble is invariably nine years. Friends and neighbors, our time is up. 1966 plus nine equals 1975 of blessed memory. The hard rain has fallen. The shitstorm has finally blown over and we have all survived to tell the tale.

Pinball, continued from page 61

All the different machines have a different "game" but each maker has a general style you can spot. Williams is usually pretty simple, with bumpers at the top with mostly simple targets positioned around the table. One thing I do like about their machines is that they have a gate where the ball will go back to the plunger lane (on a side drain) when you manage to get the gate open. That's cool. On some of Gottlieb's machines you have a post that comes up in between the two flippers and blocks the straight drain when you hit the right targets. One of the best tricks on a "post" game is to tap the flipper when you've caught a ball just enough to make it twitch and then pass the ball over the post to the other flipper. On machines like "Eight Ball" this gets you ready up for those shots on drop targets. Do it right and you'll rack up the points.

Right now the coolest machines are the Bally tables. It's really challenging to get a lot of replays on Bally's "Circus" because most of the action is up at the top of the table. It's good for left-handers too, because the bumpers and targets are exactly the same on both sides. "Hi-Lo Ace" is based on Blackjack, so you're always trying to hit twenty-one to get a Special going. Now they've even got a "Tommy"

machine which has a new type of lane that flips over four individual signs to stack up for the Special. Elton John has got one named after him called "Captain Fantastic." Too bad he can't get a hit anymore because this machine and his soccer team will probably be the way he's remembered when he quits making records. I don't know why The Who didn't get their name on a machine with their song being a hit record (twice), but maybe it's because they don't look colorful enough like Kiss or something. Or maybe it's because of that scene in their "Tommy" movie where all those machines get smashed up... What a tilt!

When it comes to tilting, every machine will do it — some are just touchier than others. On the fifth ball of a bad game sometime, shake the machine a lot to see how hard you can push it before you tilt. You can do it when the ball's draining and all you will lose are your bonuses. Watch out though because some of the older machines will kill your whole game if you do it on an early ball. Shaking front to back (as opposed to side to side), is alright, especially when the ball is up near the top, but don't try to pull it to the side when the ball's headed for the drain; it never works. When a ball hits a Gottlieb's drop target, they

will sometimes go down better with a little shake of the table.

Most machines have some kind of theme, but underneath that is usually some combination of the basic targets and drains. "Old Chicago" has gangsters, "Baseball" has home runs and strikeouts, "Twenty-one" and "Hi-Lo Ace" are based on card games, "Eight Ball" has pool rules and there's even a Gottlieb table with ten drop targets for pins that's supposed to be like bowling. So much for playing pinball so you don't have to be seen bowling...

Every player has his favorite table, and mine is definitely the "Fireball." Bally got it right on this one. It's a four-player machine, and it has a spinning "turntable" with grooves right in the middle of the table that messes with the ball so you never know which direction it'll fly off of. It's also got one of the best Specials of any table I've ever played. There're two sockets near the top where you can shoot the ball into, but it will keep that ball and give you another one to play. If you fill up both sockets, then you can hit small bumpers on either side that "release" the balls so you can have more than one ball going at once. They call them "Wotan" and "Odin," which are like some kind of German mythology gods or some-

thing. If you hit the right button off the turntable, it turns on "kickers" that won't let you side drain. If you do it just right, the two flippers still move together and the balls can't even straight drain! The best is when you get all three balls going at once and none of them can go down the drain. It's a speedy table that can give you an incredible rush. Whatta high!!

There is one thing about the state of pinball I don't like. "Fireball" and some of the other tables show that pinball is getting better than ever, but I don't know what they're trying to do with this new junk with bumpers and red electric LED's on the score. You've probably seen them—like the "Evel Knievel" table. Those space letters belong on a Texas Instruments calculator and not on a real pinball machine. It beeps, like it's "pong" or something! And by the way, watch out for the lame sell out tables like the "Spirit of '76". Another Buycentennial flop. Hey man the balls don't even klop! Let's hope that they come to their senses after the Bicentennial's over and Evel Knievel gets shown for the rip-off artist he is — and those manufacturers pick up where they left off by continuing the fine tradition of pinball machines like the "Fireball" and "Captain Fantastic."

Poised and posed, Lee's couple voted "Most Likely to Hang Out and Wait for Something to Happen" (Sean Bootkiss and Delilah 'Chutney' Bartlett) are caught in the act.

Gilligan, continued from page 53

30. Evil Doctor Mind Switch
31. Evil Doctor Hypno-ring
32. Old Growing Meteor
33. Bald Castaways
34. James "Gilligan" Bond
35. Missing Islanders Food Fangs Hyde
36. Kidnapped Castaways Coming Out Party
37. Sheriff Skipper
38. Suicidal Skipper; Admiral Gilligan
39. Quiz Show Fake Money
40. Native Girlfriend Dead Gilligan

Lonely, continued from pg. 65

and that he can stop all the ugliness caused by the dark forces lurking in the city. He even tries to rescue a 13 year-old hooker (played by Jodie Foster) from the clutches of her slimy pimp (played by Harvey Keitel). Someone who sees this movie might say, "Well, New York is such a horrible, evil place, anyway. It's no wonder that Travis Bickle's sick nightmare could occur." True, New York City can be a dangerous jungle full of terrible people. But, the fact of the matter is, the pain of loneliness, rejection, and isolation that motivates Travis to do the things he does in the movie can happen to anyone anywhere — be it in the big city, or in a small place like our town. If the pain becomes too much to bear, then something's got to give, and it's usually one's sanity. There are a lot of little cliques in this school, and there are many times that I've felt like I'm on the outside looking in because I don't "fit in" to any of them. Sometimes, I get lonely when Friday or Saturday night rolls around, and I know that there's always a party somewhere, and I'm not invited because I'm an "outsider." But, I realize that I'm lucky in the long run. I have the love of my family and a couple of close friends to keep me sane and happy. However, others who are lonely outsiders may not be so lucky. So, some parting words of wisdom to the cliquey crowd: It's easier to remove someone's loneliness by making a new friend and including them in your group, than to reject them and have a real-life Travis Bickle on your hands.

Rock Quiz Answers, from pg. 75

1. C	11. B.	21. A
2. B	12. C	22. D
3. D	13. B	23. C
4. A	14. A	24. A
5. B	15. B	25. C
6. D	16. D	26. B
7. D	17. D	27. C
8. B	18. C	28. D
9. A	19. B	29. C
10. C	20. B	30. C

American Dream, continued from pg. 84

American dream is alive and well, and I see examples of it everyday our in own generation's pursuit of it. For some, it comes in the form of a shiny, brand new 1976 Camaro or Firebird. For others, it's a date for Saturday night, or going steady with that special someone. It's also seen in the feverish try-outs for student council or head cheerleader. But, what about when we're finished with college and become real adults? Will some of us become so ambitious, reach our desired goal in life, and remain satisfied? Or will some become like the Haven Hamilton character from *NASHVILLE*, and continue to greedily reach for the brass ring of success? Will some of us become so successful in achieving our goals that it all becomes too much to bear — like the Barbara Jean character in the movie, who can barely get out of bed and perform for her fans due to "exhaustion"? Will some of us "sell out" for the sake of success at the expense of our ethnicity or race — like the black character in the movie who is a C & W star named Tommy Brown? Or will some of us, especially as women, be forced to exploit our bodies as a way to achieve success — like the Sue-Lene character? No one can predict the future in regards to the American dream and our generation. But, *NASHVILLE* is a good medium to gather food for thought on this important subject.

Departure from Vietnam, from pg. 85

were already full of passengers, but people were trying to swim out to them anyway.

"I could see people drown when they tried to get to the ships. There was a bad undertow," Lien said.

"I got a ride on a fishing boat out to one of the ships. There were so many people crowded on the deck. There were arms and legs sticking in the air out of the crowds, waving because they were being smothered to death. The South Vietnamese soldiers shot people who got in their way, and they were supposed to be on our side! I saw a bunch of them rape a woman right in front of me.

"Then I got together with a couple of young men who had stolen a rubber lifeboat. It was the kind that fills with air when you pull a cord. We jumped over the side and took the boat down the coast. When I got into the city, it was chaos all around me. Everybody was in madness, going crazy trying to get out or looting shops. There was raping and killing there, too."

Lien's parents had been killed two years before when they were visiting cousins in a village targeted by the US. Army for "pacification." Her older brother left to fight with the Viet Cong. Lien thinks he is still alive but doesn't know where to reach him.

With no family to find in Da Nang, Lien headed straight for the airport. "One of the last helicopters to leave took off while I was going to the airport. I could see people hanging onto the bottom as it raised into the air, and then fell down to their death," she said.

"It took me until night to get to the airport because of the chaos. When I got there, I found out the last airplane had left. But there were people there who wouldn't believe the Americans who they worked for would just leave them behind. We waited while the rain began falling, all night long. We wondered if anybody was coming after all, and thousands of people gathered by the edge of the runway. I thought the North Vietnamese would be there any second.

"Right after dawn, a plane came in. I ran as hard as I could: this was a race I had to win. I saw some British TV men get run over by the crowd. So many people jammed into the plane, I can't believe it took off. I was near a window, and I could see North Vietnamese rockets hit the runway after we took off."

Fortunately, Lien found an Army officer in Saigon whom she had met while working in a Da Nang hospital. He told her about an emergency program that allowed foreigners to adopt Vietnamese citizens and get them out quickly, before Saigon fell to the North Vietnamese. She met Chaney and Becky Hall, who had flown in from their vacation in Hong Kong. They had heard from a friend in the diplomatic corps about the desperate situation in Saigon, and wanted to help.

"I was very lucky," Lien said.

"I am happy I got out and happy I am in America. Life in Vietnam is hard now, it is a very poor country. But I still feel sorrow for all the people who worked for Americans but could not leave, and the people who died trying to leave. I will never forget that sad time at the end of the war."

Straight Talk, continued from page 95

Jones falls below 500, those Arabs'll be picking their face out of the sand, rug or no rug. Yes, you, near the front?

Q. Sir, it has been observed that since your inauguration, you appear to be handled by some public relations service whose apparent intention is to present you to the American people as a potato. Can you comment on this?

A. Let me try and answer this "trick" question as cleverly as I know how. From the moment it became clear that my great predecessor was to be unfairly hounded from office in totally deserved disgrace, I decided I would present myself to the American people watching me on the other end of this big metal gismo and all those suave foreigners as something familiar, friendly, and basic — in short, a potato.

Accordingly, I turned, as I always do in every situation short of putting one foot in front of the other, to the Vice-President. In the course of a vigorous heart-to-heart with him and the aid of some invigorating little pills he carries, he convinced me that I was already, without the help of some New York, aviator-glasses, high-heeled cream puff, a bona fide vegetable. Or, more precisely, a tuber.

And in that role I am willing to go to the ends of the earth to bring peace to the planet. I am even willing, if necessary, to stay there. Thank you. Thank you. Thank you very much. Thank you. Look, I've got to, thank you, but really — thank you — got to — oh, forget it. And thank you.

124

Turning Pot into Hash, continued from page 49

smoke of any kind stop cooking! Because you're probably vaporizing oil and not alcohol. Well you're done. And now you should have a dark oil the consistency of honey. Wow!! This shit is cool, huh?!?! Store it in glass vials.

5. Before we go into variations lets smoke a little of the dope we got!! First you need a hash oil pipe. Available at any head shop. This is a glass pipe with a bubble bowl at the end. Put about three drops in the bowl and heat from the bottom with a flame till it starts to boil. Where there's fire there's smoke. So when you see some take a toke. While you turn off the heat. Enjoy.

Variations

Isomerize-isomerization is actually a chemical process that releases the psychoactive properties of THC that are sometimes too bound molecularly to be effective (Dirtweed). If you have some really good pot like Red Bud Columbian, Acapulco Gold, Oaxican or Sensemilia, you won't want to compromise the taste of your oil with this procedure.

1. To isomerize you'll need about a 1/4 cup of sulfuric acid and a 1/2 cup of baking soda. Follow the usual procedures up to the part where you remove the pot grinds. At this point, instead of throwing them away save the grounds.

2. Pour the acid into bottom and mix a bit. (You should remove about half the alcohol before starting this.) Put the top on and set ISO on low. Let it cook for about two hours. Let it cool and then pour in the baking soda to neutralize the acid. Stir a bit.

3. Add the old pot grinds to soak up the alcohol and oil. When all the oil is thoroughly soaked back into pot, remove and put it in cheesecloth or something you can run water through to wash off baking soda without losing pot.

4. When soda is completely gone put grounds back in filter. Repeat extraction process with alcohol (it should go much faster now that the pot has been used once) and follow usual procedure to create oil.

Hash - Proceed till you have all the oil and alcohol in the bottom. Now take fresh pot, grind it up. Remove about 3/4 alcohol from the mixture and then add pot. When thoroughly soaked, set on low with the top off, stir two or three times as the alcohol evaporates. Then right before it is totally dry scoop it out. Put on some parchment or baking paper. Pack flat and put on rack in oven. You may not even have to turn the oven on. If it's not warm and dry enough, turn it on as low as it will go and leave in for a few hours or until dry.

Simple enough? One last note; if you use the steps and concepts I'm talkin' about you can really make your own distilling "box" you know, like moonshine during the depression. Go for the gold...

516

abzug

abzug ('ab-zug) *n.* : a violent eruption, such as from a volcano. (*Run for your lives or the abzug will get us!*)

agnew ('ag-nū) *v.i.* : to turn out differently than expected; to boomerang. (*The ball agnewed and hit him in the face.*)

ali (äl-'ē) *adj.* : made of clay.

brando ('bran-dō) *v.i.* : to speak incoherently; to mumble. (*Who can understand him, the way he brandos!*)

¹buckley ('buk-lē) *v.i.* : to make a succession of right turns until one returns to his original position.

²buckley *adj.* : intellectual to the point of being incomprehensible.

carson ('kar-sun) *n.* : a glib huckster. **syn.** griffin, cavett, bishop (*obs.*).

chiang (che-äng) *n.* : a small, broken fragment of antique china.

¹cosell (kō-'sel) *v.i.* : to infuriate an audience by speaking in a tiresome manner. (*He coselled until twelve million viewers turned off their sets in disgust.*)

²cosell *n.* : an inflammation of the mouth. ("*I thought it might be strep, but it's only a cosell,*" the doctor said.)

eagleton ('ē-gul-tun) *n.* : anything supported one thousand per cent.

faisal ('fī-zul) *n.* : an energy crisis. (*We can't turn on the lights, baby, because of the faisal.*)

fischer ('fish-ur) *n.* : a victory without a winner.

¹fonda ('fon-duh) *n.* : a parent bewildered by the generation gap.

²fonda *v.i.* : to take a wild ride, esp. on a motorcycle.

³fonda *n.* **1:** a peace chant intoned by North Vietnamese in times of war. **2:** a war chant intoned by North Vietnamese in times of peace.

friedan (fri-'dan) *adj.* : unresponsive to the needs of man. (*His marriage, alas, was friedan and doomed.*)

getty ('get-ē) see **onassis**.

hughes (huz) *n? adj?* meaning obscure.

humphrey ('hum-frē) *v.i.* : to speak in a single breath a sentence of more than fifty words covering six or more topics. (*He humphreyed, but, as usual, no one listened.*)

irving ('ir-ving) *n.* **1:** a tall tale. **2:** a cliff-hanger.

kunstler ('kunst-lur) *n.* : a mouthpiece for blowing one's horn.

leary ('li·u-rē) *n.* : an unidentifiable flying object. (*It's a leary,*" the navigator said, "*and it's gaining on us.*")

lindsay ('lin-zē) *v.i.* : to party-hop.

liz (liz) *adj.* : split; severed; disconnected.

lovelace ('luv-lās) *n.* a union of two or more people; an unlimited partnership.

mao (mão) *n.* a Chinese staple, usually consumed with rice. (*An hour after having our mao, we were hungry again.*)

¹neuman ('nü-mun) *n.* : an expected disaster.

²neuman *adj.* : nothing. (*It was a neuman year.*)

³neuman *v.i.* to worry. (*What? Me neuman?*)

nixon ('nik-sun) *n.* **1:** a busted football play. **2:** an illness lasting six years. ("*You must let the nixon run its course,*" the doctor said.)

onassis (ō-'nas-is) *n.* : an ancient unit of wealth, five of which equal one getty.

plimpton ('plimp-[...] poorly somethin[...] thought he was [...] could do was p[...]

puzo ('pū-zō) *n.* [...] to refuse. (*The [...] told him it was [...]*

rainier (ran-'yā) [...] grace.

redgrave ('red-g[...] of English bir[...] mating habits.

riggs (rigs) *n.* **1[...]** ator. **2:** an o[...] throne of a ki[...] to the riggs, [...]

roth (rōth) *n.* [...]

sadat (sä-'dät) [...] desert, which [...] nowhere. (*Ge[...] it's only a sad[...]*

schulz (shulz) [...] one who wo[...]

spitz (spits) *v.* [...] self. (*While [...] he spitzed.*)

spock (spok) [...] spoiled child [...] you can sa[...] Street.*")

susskind ('sus[...] difficult to s[...]

tim (tim) *n.* **1** [...] **2:** a female[...]

unitas (ü-'nī[...] to pasture. [...]

wayne (wān[...]

welch (welc[...] chest. (*Her [...] through th[...]*

welk (welk) [...] where we [...] flat.)

Man, what's the deal with Ford? Bullets flying at him twice in one month. Granted, he's no angel, but he beats the heck out of old Tricky Dick Nixon. Seriously; the WIN buttons were really stupid, but they're hardly a reason to off the guy. Besides, Ford is a real cool comedian, what with his tripping all the time, or trying to eat tamales with the corn shucks still on them. Lyndon Baines Johnson once said Ford's stupidity was due to the fact that he must have played a lot of football without wearing a helmet. Far-out, man.

Of course Squeaky's personal bitch with Ford makes little sense. It had to do with Manson's hatred of Nixon, who he blamed for "the Family's" demise. Man, it's ironic — Squeaky tried to kill Ford as he was on his way to address the California Legislature about starting a nationwide effort to curb violent crime, including stricter gun control measures. What a trip!

Speaking of Squeaky, there are a lot of similarities between her and Tania. Both dug sex-crazed egotistical dudes who predicted heavy stuff, man — like the end of the world was coming down soon because of race wars. Both came from families with tons of bread (and probably had some kink of freaky competition thing going on with their mommies). Both made it a point to use the word "pigs" as often as possible when rapping about the establishment.

And what's the food thing? All these chicks had a weird association with food. When she was busted, Squeaky had the munchies for ice cream. The New York Times reported that when Tania was busted, she was constantly chewing gum and looked more like someone "who would have remained unnoticed in an all-night cafeteria than a millionaire heiress." Freaky, man.

Then of course, there's that thing about the SLA demanding food for the poor, and Randolph Hearst establishing the People In Need program, which by the way, donated $2 million worth of food. Man check this out — did you know Sara Jane not only briefly worked for Daddy Hearst's paper, The San Francisco Examiner, but also volunteered for the People In Need program. Or that Sara Jane and Tania shared the same corridor at the federal prison in San Mateo County, but sat at different tables for their meals? Or that when Sara Jane and Charles Manson were kids in Charleston, West Virginia, they used to buy candy from the same grocer? Man it's like there's some cosmic connection or maybe it some sort of conspiracy... another connection is big weapons — Squeaky with a .45 caliber semi-automatic, Tania with a machine gun, and Sara Jane, with a .38 caliber handgun. Funny, after being busted, Sara Jane said, referring to Ford, "If I had had my .44, I would have caught him."

Man, what the hell are these chicks doing with guns that big, anyway? They should've been packing something more their size. Remember that cute red gun Barbara Feldon used to carry around on Get Smart? Girls shouldn't be carrying big guns, because I think it makes them freak out. I tell you, it's hormones gone haywire combined with that wild, free, and crazy northern California thing. But thanks to those wacky hormones, these girls are crazy even without the guns. Squeaky wears a stupid cloak as part of some dumb worship of Manson and carved an X in her forehead to X herself out of the system. Need I say more? Tania, who'd probably been forced to cop too much acid by the SLA in their attempts to brainwash her, wet her panties when the FBI busted her, according to Newsweek. And Sara Jane — man, she's really out there. Like, she said she was glad Ford didn't die, wished she would have been caught speeding on her way to try to snuff him, and that if Ford had taken any longer to leave the hotel she "would have had to leave to pick up her son at school." Then she turns around and tells The Los Angeles Times, "I am not a berserk woman." Man, is she for real or what?

What this all comes down to is total chaos for right-thinking women who want to get ahead. Man the problem is that we have are a bunch of liberated women running around without any cool role models. Take it from me girls, do yourselves a favor before it's too late and follow in Toni Tenille's footsteps.

The young and haughty senior Karen Metchel was recently crowned "Queen of the Heartbreakers." Her winning 32 boykills sets a new R.E. Lee record! Way to go, KM! Practice makes perfect.

CONTRIBUTORS

EDITOR/ART DIRECTOR:
DENISE MONTGOMERY

DESIGN:
ERIK JOSOWITZ , ZERO-G

PRODUCTION COORDINATOR:
TRICIA LINKLATER

PRODUCTION ASSISTANTS:
RON MARKS, KATHY KLINE, BRENT BUFORD, BENJAMIN KOSNICK, SHANNA CLESTER, PAUL JOHNSON, CATHIE HUTCHINS, GREG HERVEY, BOB PRESTWOOD, CHRISTI BACOT-LIAISON PRODUCTION SERVICES, LARRY JOLLY, NAN MELTZER, DEB LEWIS, COURTNEY ELDRIDGE, TRACY WEAVER, AND DEBBIE PASTOR

An excited Lee Yearbook staff after hearing the good news: there WILL be an actual class sponsored field trip!!! Until recent developments the anxious gang was going to "trip in a field" and call it a done deal. Praise the "higher powers!"

WRITERS
(in alphabetical order)

MELANIE ARMSTRONG:
"Word search Puzzle"

BILL BLANCHARD:
"New Sports Hero"

PAMELA BRUCE:
Movie Reviews: "Dubious Disaster Films", "The Devil Still Makes Hollywood Do It", "Only the Lonely", "The American Dream" and "Who's Really in Control"; Male celebrity profiles: John Travolta, Starsky and Hutch, Freddie Prinze, Lee Majors, Telly Savalas, Burt Reynolds, and Warren Beatty; "A Dazed and Confused Timeline"

GARY CHESTER:
"Letter to a Friend "

SHANNA CLESTER:
"Michelle's Better Crocked Brownies"

BILL DANIEL:
"Why Art is Important to Good Citizenship"

LEE DANIEL:
Car Profiles: "The Boogie Van", "Melba toast" "The Judge", and "The Grey Ghost"

KIETH FLETCHER:
"Comedy tonight"; "A Rock'n'Roll Trivia Quiz"

ROBERT JACKS:
"TV talk"

LYNN KELLER:
"Classroom Notes"

KIM KRIZAN:
"We Need the ERA now"; "Ms. Stroud's Stolen Diary"

RICHARD LINKLATER:
"Still Dazed After All These Years"

TRICIA LINKLATER:
"Shoes News Now"; "Typical Dude Diagram"; "Foxy fashions"

SETH MAXWELL MALICE:
"Skyrockets in Flight, Afternoon Delight!"; "101 Ways to Smoke Pot at School"; "What the Bicentennial Means to Me"; "What the Bicentennial means to us"; "Helpful hints from Shavonne: Ten Ways to Open a Beer without an Opener"; "I Don't Know What You Are Talkin' about Dad"; "The Downing of the SS. Minnow"; "Helpful Hints by Benny: What to Do When You have a Substitute Teacher"; "Helpful Hints from Wooderson: Pot Etiquette"; "Helpful Hints by Michelle: Roach Clips Under Pressure"

BILLY PRINGLE:
"Turning Pot into Hash"; "Zen and the Art of Playing Foosball"

JOHN SLATE:
"Melvin Spivey's Top Ten"

R.U. STIENBERG:
Women celebrity profiles: Lindsey Wagner, Farrah Fawcett Majors, Cher Bono, and Barbra Streisand; "Gun Toting Dames are a Bummer and Must Be Stopped"; "A Dazed and Confused Time Line" (with Pamela Bruce)

CANDI STRECKER:
"The Friendly Fraternity of Freaks"

RANDY "BISCUIT" TURNER:
"Go Ask Darla"

TODD WALKER:
"Pinball Flippers and Kickers and other Helpful Hints"; "Tips on How to Play the Fireball"

CHRIS WALTERS:
"Profiles in Confusion" (with Bill Wise); "What Watergate Means to Me"; "The First Anniversary of Saigon's Fall"

BILL WISE
All advertising spoofs and photo captions; "Who's Where, Who's There"; "Profiles in Confusion" (with Chris Walters); "Basic Trade and Industrial Education";"It's a Smoked World After All"; "Spirit of '76"; "Helpful Hints: What to Do When You Have a Substitute Teacher "What's in Pickford's Locker"; "How to Keep that Old L.P. Playing Long"; " Intro to Melvin Spivey's Top 10"; "How to Pick Up Girls book report"; "Don Dawson's book report", "Bruno's pot slang"

PHOTOGRAPHERS
(in alphabetical order)

ANTHONY RAPP:
"Lee high school hallway" pg. 22, &"The four crisscross girls " pg. 88

GABOR SZITANYI: The high school yearbook photos and most of the stills from the movie Dazed and Confused.

ROMAN TRACY:
"The Judge" pg. 52
'The Fireball', pgs. 60-61

KIMBERLY WRIGHT:
"Shoe news now" pg. 45, and
"Foxey Fashions" pgs. 67-68

PHOTO COLLAGES
RON MARKS:
"Creem 1975 reader's poll" pgs. 30-31

BRENT BUFORD:
"Failure is it's own reward" pg.40-41; "Gun toting dames are a bummer and must be stopped" pg. 89

CARTOONS/DRAWINGS
ANDY BLACKWOOD:
Political cartoons pg. 42

JERRY DOG:
Pot rolling drawings pgs. 38-39

Additional thanks— to Robin Harrington, Emily Marshall and Chaim Magnum at REMIX in L.A. and Nathali Jensen At ROOTS in Beverly Hills for supplying shoes for "Shoe News Now"

Additional thanks— to David Drader, Marissa Ribisi, And Gina Ribisi at MONSTER in North Hollywood for supplying most of the wardrobe for "Foxy Fashions"

Stay cool.
See you next year.